Searching
for
"It"

Searching for "It"

Fifty Years of
Conversation *with the*
Road Warrior Therapist

Ken Ludmer

ARCHWAY
PUBLISHING

Archway Publishing books may be ordered through booksellers or by contacting:

Archway Publishing
1663 Liberty Drive
Bloomington, IN 47403
www.archwaypublishing.com
1 (888) 242-5904

ISBN: 978-1-4808-8766-4 (sc)
ISBN: 978-1-4808-8767-1 (e)

Library of Congress Control Number: 2020905176

Print information available on the last page.

Archway Publishing rev. date: 5/6/2020

Dedication

When I started to write this book, I had to think of all the people who contributed to my quest to define "it". The task was a bit overwhelming. My search began at age fifteen at the Figaro Café in Greenwich Village, where I saw men in casual dress, sitting around reading the Village Voice, drinking coffee, and talking about "it" in film, theatre, travel, books, and life experience. As I talked with them, a whole new world opened up. There was now, for me, an alternative to wearing a tie and getting an office job uptown. This search for knowledge eventually led me to travel to forty countries. It also was responsible for my hitchhiking across America twice and throughout Europe and North Africa to gather the road experience that Kerouac and others said was mandatory for a young man seeking answers. I had the Woody Guthrie songs in my head, and I wanted to travel those roads.

I want to dedicate this collection of my stories and experiences to all the men and women whom I met and talked with along the way: the truckers, waitresses, farmers, traveling salesmen, scouts, store owners, cowboys, cops, gamblers, ranchers, teachers, and others who reached out to me and offered conversations, opinions, and observations to a person who was searching for meaning in a confusing and at times conflicted life. The people I talked to were from every walk of life. I met them everywhere—on the road, in the classroom, in any place where I paused to sit down and have a friendly chat about life and what it means. It is these people to whom I dedicate this book, because they offered me a path where I saw none, a challenge where I needed one, and a way of looking at life that opened doors to new thinking.

Acknowledgments

To all my students, teachers, friends, clients, and colleagues I want to say thank you. I hope you find yourself in this book. You are woven into the fabric of my story and have been essential to my growth as a person. I offer this collection of life experience as a way of acknowledging that every single conversation can potentially be life-changing. The desire to understand "It" is universal and the opinions about its meaning are as diverse and contradictory as the human condition itself. I offer mine in the hope that maybe you, the reader, will see yourself in these stories and benefit as I have from hearing about others and their quests to find "it".

For the book itself, I am lucky to have collaborated with the very talented, super smart, perceptive, and knowledgeable Krista Hill, my editor, whom I trusted to guide me with this story. She and I formed a spiritual bond where humor knew no bounds. We laughed and shared our experiences and I hope our result will bring some enjoyment and insights, and maybe a laugh or two. She was a joy to work with and I offer her a heads up: I have more stories to tell!

Contents

Introduction

What is "It"?

When I retired as a therapist, the first change I noticed was that I missed teaching and supervising. To me, it felt like a void, being that I had a whole bunch of knowledge and experience and I wasn't using it to help others. I asked myself how I could best impart some of it to students or other therapists with less experience. I thought of institutes where I could commit to supervision of a class. I thought of getting back on the lecture and workshop circuit. I finally thought that a book would be best.

The next thought was that the book didn't only have to be about students and therapists. Everyone needs a mentor—I certainly did. So, I asked myself, "How do I tell 'it'?" That only brought up the question "What is it?" Then, the light bulb lit. First, I had to pose the questions about what "it" was and then try to answer them.

This book is an attempt to impart what I have learned along life's many paths. Knowledge comes from many different sources and experiences and I offer this collection of stories and experiences as one possible way for readers to ponder the concept of "it"—and enjoy a laugh or two.

So, what is "it"? "It" is always tough to define. Let's start with the basics. "It" is a neutral pronoun. That's the easy part. Some people have it, others don't. Some people get it, others don't. "It" can be everything or nothing. One thing, though, is true: everyone is looking for "it". A capitalist and a monk both want it; they just take different roads to find it. I doubt that anyone gets on the right road at first. That's what growing up is all about. You go down the wrong road and it can be many more wrong roads before you change direction and find one more suited to what you really need, rather than what you want. How many songs are about that? The happiest people like having what they *need*, as opposed to others who keep searching for what they *like* or *want*.

Many of these roads are mirages. You think you have found "it", but somehow it doesn't last. Take passion and heat in first encounters, for example. How many rocket-shot romances have you seen where everything is magical, the sex is intense and all-consuming, and then things fade away. In the view of therapists, it's a common phenomenon. People project onto others what they need and take it as truth because it feels familiar and safe. Later, when you really see the other person and not just your projected self, there is a lessening of intensity when reality seeps in. Then, you are back on the road to repeat it all over again.

How many men spend years lifting skirts, looking for "it"? I'd venture most American men have been trained to look there. We glamorize women, idolize them with all the "image" clothing, and then spend endless hours in pursuit of the prize underneath. Women feed into the belief that they are the prize. They are sold billions of dollars of products from shoes to handbags, clothing to hairstyles, makeup, nail polish, perfume and so on, just to present themselves as the prize. How many women's magazines, blogs, and books tell young women what the proper amount of time is before the prize can be revealed? Look at all that preparation and dancing to the script of romance, only to find that you didn't find "it" when you thought you had it.

There is natural curiosity before all this packaging takes over. "Playing doctor" is a kid's way to get a look. "Playing house" is doing what your parents did, and depending on what the hell was going on in your house, it could be a very dicey game. Sex is probably the most written-about topic as it plays out in life's unfolding dramas: in books, on stage, and in films. No wonder when you get a turn at it, you have no idea what it is you should do, or if what someone told you to do is right. When I saw my first vagina, I was stunned as the line was not horizontal but vertical. Who knew? Finding it depends on defining what "it" is. We could start by saying it's really all about understanding. Understanding *what*, you say? Well, in short, everything.

To a bridge cable worker, "it" is an uncanny ability to focus and overcome inborn fears. To a guru, "it" is everything combined into one formula. To a soldier, "it" is the ability to see, feel, and react without hesitation to maintain self-preservation. To an animal trainer, "it" is the connecting to innate sensors that instill calm in the face of fear. For a therapist, "it" is a combination of art and science that leads to deeper understanding of people and their behaviors. Like most acquired skills, "it" has a knowledge base that has theories and beliefs. For healers, "it" includes a deep sensitivity to the human condition, backed by years of testing, change, and personal growth. Easy stuff, right?

I know people who didn't want "it". It was either too difficult or too easy for them. They instead would take whatever came along. What is "it" to an artist? How many paintings before you can say you have "it"? What is "it" to a Buddhist? How long do you meditate until you feel it? When can you say you have it under control?

For all of us, it begins with a want. Then, it morphs into something else. There may be detours, roadblocks, and outright walls. Up hills and down hills. Small successes, followed by failures, and vice versa. The bottom line is, if you want "it", no matter what it is, be prepared for a long, dedicated journey.

When I was teaching graduate psychiatric social work to students from Columbia and Yeshiva Universities in a Community Mental Health Center's Department of Psychiatry, they would ask a direct and simple question: "How do you learn 'it'"? The "it" being how to understand what comprises the entire knowledge base of being a therapist. At the time, I would answer, "It's just like a musician and his or her dream of Carnegie Hall: practice, practice, practice!" Over the years, my answer would change, and I would add, "Get lots of life experience". Later, I told them, "Know yourself, and be, rather than wish", and "Listen with a caring heart". The list kept getting longer and longer as the years rolled by.

There is no substitute for learning your craft, which means reading everything and getting top-notch, live clinical supervision—in front of a one-way mirror—from the best in the field. I got mine from Salvador Minuchin, and his teaching staff, who watched my live sessions at the Child Guidance Clinic at the Children's Hospital of Philadelphia.

Here's what it was like: In the session, there would be a family and myself, with the ominous one-way mirror and the full supervising staff observing on the other side. There also was the dreaded phone on the wall, connected to the staff, and you were mandated to answer it immediately when it rang during the session. When it sounded, chills went up the spine. The observing Minuchin would say, "You can't hear anything if you are talking." Other times, he would say, "Did you notice their bodies weren't saying what their words were saying?" Or, he would intone "Empathy is felt—give some."

As I learned how to listen, what I said became more caring as I cut through the words to get to the soul of the matter. His voice is still in my head: "You are a healer—find the pain and ease it. Forget the book, reach out and hold a hand."

When I graduated from Columbia University, my Department Chair gave me a book. "You will need this, too," she said as she handed it to me. It was Robert Pirsig's *Zen and the Art of Motorcycle Maintenance*. It made perfect sense to my Aquarian soul: while your head is in the clouds, make sure your feet are firmly planted on the ground. I had learned that lesson years before on my first LSD trip. A group of us were at Fire Island beach on Long Island's south shore on a late spring day when I dropped my first tab. My mind expanded exponentially as I counted the grains of sand in one hand and wondered how many there were. Why were they all different? How many on the entire south shore? Or in the world? Realizing the immenseness of it all, while knowing I was just one grain of sand in all of time, amid all this vastness, was fascinating to my newly discovered, limitless thinking. I was consumed with the thought.

I spent the entire day letting my mind go where it wanted. Watching waves go by from the end of the island was a new phenomenon. When had I ever seen a wave go by and not risen with it? I also had some thoughts about how many gallons of water were in the ocean. Then, there were the birds and the crawly things that scattered back into the water. You get the idea—it was a busy day in my head. By the end of the day, I had second degree sunburn because I had paid no attention. Lesson learned. You can let your mind wander solving all kinds of problems, but your body is here on this planet, under a hot sun. Both need care.

Here we are, fifty years later, and to answer any new students' basic questions I have compiled a list of lessons learned from travels and talks with everyone from everywhere—about forty countries' worth—plus, a few hundred books and five thousand movies. I will count only one hundred plays, endless lectures, and workshops. Television? Forget it. I'll just say you can learn from it. Oh, and one more thing: fifty years of therapy sessions and weekly supervision. *Damn, there's more* … Teaching hundreds of students and answering ten thousand questions—and don't forget school. You can learn there, if you go to a good one and have great mentors. I was lucky. Put it all together and meditate on it. Then, read all your notes and try to write a book.

I need to add just one more thing: listen to everyone at the top, and everyone at the bottom. They know stuff. The list should help you find "it".

Here goes ... oh, one more thing: you have to *want* to.

Pain and Loss

There is no greater teacher than what is contained in these two words. Some believe it is the core of what makes people change. When you experience it, you have a choice: learn from it or repeat it.

I was sixteen when my father dropped dead. My mother was totally swept up by a major depression and I was left to fend for myself. Within a month, I was awakened nightly by bizarre, traumatic dreams that were both scary and violent. I wanted to know how to interpret their meaning. I was never known to be that way and these dreams were making me afraid to go to sleep.

I went to the NYC Public Library and fumbled my way through the card catalogue, eventually finding a book entitled *The Interpretation of Dreams* by Sigmund Freud. *Never heard of him.* I filled out the slip and handed it in. The librarian then gave me a card with a number on it and said, "Look at the board, and when your number lights up, your book will be here at the desk." I felt so adult-like as I looked at the long tables filled with serious-looking people reading and writing. When my number lit up, the librarian handed me this very formal-looking book. I sat down and started to read—not knowing I was embarking on my journey to becoming a therapist.

From what my young mind could understand, there was a vast system of symbolic messages located deep within me that existed in a continuum known as the "unconscious". My dreams came from this untapped reservoir of fears, anxieties, hopes, and desires. After weeks of reading, I started to make some sense of my dreams and, after a while, I could categorize them as what had already happened to me, and what I wanted to happen to me. Some reflected my fears of what *could* happen to me. None of them were fun.

I learned about ego defenses. I could now define *denial, projection, displacement, reaction formation, sublimation,* and *identification* and differentiate them from simple wants and needs. I learned about the primary drives for survival, both aggressive and sexual. The more I learned, the more I wanted to dream, as it was the key to what was going on within me. I found out I was merely a scared-out-of-my-mind teenager who had suffered a trauma and was full of resulting fears about my own future. I was angry that I had lost two parents in one day and had no way to express it verbally as there was no one to talk to. Freud helped me see what was underneath—and it all made sense. My dreams were breakthroughs into my conscious world and they should have stayed below. My problem was that I did not have a strong enough protective barrier to keep my unconscious "unconscious". I wasn't alone, as Freud was describing a human condition. Knowing I was only scared and not crazy made a world of difference. Reading and learning were ways to help myself. I also saw that we all lived at two levels simultaneously. Some people had better boundaries than others. A lot of people were vulnerable like me.

There would be a lot to learn, but I already felt I was onto something very big. I was sixteen and dealing with my unconscious. Everybody else was watching Dick Clark on *American Bandstand*. What was the lesson? I learned that I could learn. It helped me trust myself. I had just figured out something that was very big, and it was what I needed.

Ray Charles also helped. It was a tough year for me, and I also discovered that music touched the soul. I now had Sigmund for my dreams and Ray to help me get there. I was on my way.

Learning "It" From Women

There were so many women I learned from, but the one that started the ball rolling was my maternal grand-mother, Nanny. She was my savior, the warm, generous, ever-trusting woman who gave unconditional love. I lived with her when I was five while my father recuperated from his heart attack in Florida. I also spent summers with her and Pop-Pop at Mombasha Lake, in Bear Mountain, where we lived in a primitive bungalow.

Time with Nanny was special because she took an interest in me and loved to teach me. We cooked together as I helped her with the vegetables and the potatoes. We baked pies and cookies. We played cards every day. We would sit together in one big chair at the lake at night and gaze at the stars and she would tell stories of her childhood in Hanover, Germany. She would come to the porch where I slept on a cot and scratch my back until I fell asleep.

Nanny taught me to be kind, in thought and in action. We rescued injured animals all the time. We painted pictures. She always said it was easier to be good than angry. I learned that, if you give first, then good things happened. She loved when it rained and told me about all the beneficial things that would happen because of it, like the plants and vegetables growing and the animals having fresh water to drink. No dark clouds for her—she was a positive person and her goodness is what I think of when I think of her.

Nanny told me I was a very sensitive boy and that when I grew up I would need to find a good woman who would love me and not take advantage of my soft side. She was right.

My early attempts at relationships were imbalanced: I gave too much without reciprocal return. Nanny's message had been simple and direct: "You know how to love and in order for it to work, you will need to receive the same as well."

We had Thanksgiving at Nanny's every year, and the warmth of those meals is one of my strongest memories of her. She would serve a huge meal and I always helped make the stuffing. To this day, I use her recipe.

"It", to Nanny, was love. She maintained that life was not the same without it. Nanny never had money, fame, or a lot of possessions, but she was a happy woman who was loved as a good person should be—especially by me.

So, how does one learn what 'it' is with women when love

and sex are involved? How many books are there on that subject? I learned that there must be balance for any relationship to work. If one is doing all the giving, emotionally or physically, the partnership will fail. The rock-bottom, number one necessity is trust. One cannot build a relationship if you have one eye looking for betrayal or one foot out the door. So many women have been burned by men who said one thing to them and did another. I saw many women in treatment who said they were lied to and cheated on by men who said they loved them. It goes the other way as well.

So, if "it" begins with trust, what comes next? The next step usually has to do with balance, or as others say, control. Who controls the relationship? Who tends to its needs and makes sure that communication and decision-making are balanced? Hopefully, the answer is both persons.

During the various stages of dating, the lessons come rather frequently. Not everyone is healthy emotionally, and if you happen to get your pheromones interlocked with someone, shall we say, less stable then they should be, well, the ride is going to get bumpy. When two people experience a hot or fiery connection, that is not necessarily an indication of true love, as they might initially tend to think. Heat is what it is: heat, not love. So many couples rely on the physical aspect of their relationship to solve all their conflicts. "Make-up sex is the best," they say. It's not.

One doesn't have to dangle off a cliff each week to feel good about being rescued. Too much reliance on sex or making it too important is usually a sign that something else that is missing. Like emotional security, for one.

Many people have emotional abandonment issues that they believe can be cured by hot sex. It's a Band-Aid, not a cure. Sure, it feels good to be longed for passionately all the time, but the flame will cool and if you don't have the necessary supporting relationship, the fire will go out.

The lessons learned from dating are usually played out in the second major relationship. How many people who are taken advantage of are super-cautious in their next relationship? Givers hold back. Takers start to give. Often, it's timing that either brings people closer or prevents them from even beginning to know one another. How often do we hear, "It's not you, it's me." It means, "I know I'm not ready for you, but I could be in another time". Hurt takes time. So does love. Heat is now. When people try to go too fast in a relationship, it is a signal that all is not well. There is some reason a person wants to gather all the intimacy quickly, so that anxiety, which masks a deeper trust issue, doesn't come to the surface. The thinking is, "I have to lock down this relationship because I fear I can't make it without it. The timing makes one person uncomfortable and no amount of cajoling will change it. You can bake a pie faster by turning up the heat, but it will not taste the same when you rush it.

Let's talk about honesty, a major component in the world of "it" lessons. Some people lie to gain an advantage, painting a more favorable picture of themselves in order to seemingly impress the other person. That is a short-term players game, as the truth always comes out, sooner or later. Some people are lying to themselves and that is more dangerous. Look at addiction and denial when you talk about lying to yourself. How many people with good intentions have been snared in that trap: charging in and trying to save the addicted person or change them with their love? Sadly, far too many. Honesty is a sign of emotional health. Emotionally healthy people acknowledge both their strengths and their weaknesses with candor. We all strive to be better, and honest self-examination is a good place to start. Try to use a mirror that isn't cracked.

Why is it that your friends can always tell who is good for you and who isn't? It's almost uncanny how accurate a friend's evaluation can be. They don't have a blind spot when it comes assessment. Couples caught up in pheromones, needs, wishes, and desires can be very poor judges. It always comes out in time, but after a while, people get tired of making the same mistake over and over. Your friend will tell you that you are "doing it again". You should listen to the warning.

Another one of my learning "it" teachers was a black female nurse whom I met in Germany. We worked at the same hospital and she became my closest female friend. Bobbi was about five years older than I, and her no-nonsense view of the world was based on how she was treated by whites back in her home state of North Carolina, and by the military. She said the military had less prejudice and was more merit-based. In combat, everyone in uniform is your brother and skin color doesn't matter.

Bobbi and I hit it off immediately as we shared the same sense of humor. Our similarity was based on our experiences with authority and social norms. My NYC background had exposed me to all forms of power and prejudice. I could understand her fear of the police and listened to her stories of being disregarded because she was a woman or because she was black. Sometimes both.

When she talked about men, it was from a position that they all talked a good game, but she wasn't impressed with "talkers"—she was looking for "doers". Bobbi's ability to see through bullshit was like watching a laser cut through rock. She was warm, yet protective. "Got a be that way—too many people looking to get over on you." She explained how it was hard for black men to impress a woman if they were trying to do it with money or position, as most of them did not have either. For her, it came down to character and integrity.

Bobbi was such a good truth-teller when it came to people and their motives. It was like learning to see things with an X-ray machine behind your eyes. She was attractive and super-smart. Her view was that the attractive part was fine with black men, but the super-smart part caused them some difficulties. Men wanted to keep women in a certain place, and when they felt threatened, they resorted to control measures. "That just doesn't cut it with me," she would say.

I learned from Bobbi about image versus reality. The adage that "all that glitters is not gold" was one she pointed out all the time. She never worried about clothing or makeup. "What I wear is adequate," she would say. "If you want more from me, you have to look inside." Bobbi had an appreciation for men as she had three brothers. She had observed them closely as they plotted their sexual conquests. Thinking she would be in the same position as those women when she grew up, she stored the recollections of her brothers' experiences, referring to them as her "brother inventory". When men in her life began to sound like her brothers, she knew it was a strategy. More was needed to obtain her approval.

Bobbi and I talked for hours over *kaffe* in downtown Heidelberg—we did not get the disapproving stares we would have back in the

US. Germany was more advanced socially, especially in Heidelberg, where black male soldiers stayed after their tours were up and married German locals. They knew it was easier there than at home.

If you listen to a black woman explain what it's like to be on the bottom of the social scale, it is heartbreaking. Their battle begins with powerful white men and ends with powerful white men. From relationships to court, from the police to the board of directors, it's all about white men in power. Maybe today it is a bit different, but if you listen carefully to the current President, his attack mode is directed at intelligent black, Hispanic, and Muslim women who speak their minds.

Far and beyond, my best lessons were the ones I learned by running a women's therapy group: seven women and myself, discussing love, sex, relationships, attitudes, husbands, bosses, children, mothers, fathers, ethics, boundaries, abuse, health, and everything in between. We met weekly, and I had one individual session with each woman monthly. I had constant supervision, as this was one tough group. There was never a session without issues. Either the women were competitive with one another or they were combative. My goal was to get them to be supportive, and that took time and many sessions with conflict resolution as the goal.

In the beginning, they were competitive for me, which is a usual therapy norm. Then, they focused more on themselves and I became invisible, except when a different perspective was called for. I always told them that I did not represent men, as in that environment I was the therapist who represented mental health knowledge. They frequently challenged that view. Whenever they spoke disparagingly about men, they would be quick to say, "Present company exempted".

When a group finally forms and its trust issues are resolved, the openness is very powerful. It represents social norms as the usual fears of rejection and ostracization surface. Once that stage has passed, the ultimate freedom is to be able to speak your truth—and no one can take that away from you.

There were awkward and painful times when sexual abuse was the topic. I learned so much about what women think of sex—and men in general. I found out that the code among women is even stronger than the one among men. A true gender difference is men will not talk about sex with their wives to other men; they will only speak of affairs and women from their past. Women, on the other hand, have no problem talking about sex with their husbands to other women. Once we were a formed group and most of the competitive and alignment issues were out in the open, they would periodically ask me as a man and not a therapist what my opinion was. I always responded that my answer would reflect mental health thinking and not my personal thoughts. One day, they pushed very hard after they had ridiculed men's bedroom performances as woefully inadequate, self-centered, and totally laughable. They wanted to know personally if any of their discussions was difficult for me to hear. I couldn't help but chuckle and told them that I hoped that I could get it up after hearing what they had to say.

I saw men in a different light after listening to those good women. I saw vulnerability and sensitivity displayed in every session—very different from men's groups, where getting to that stage took twice as long. I saw how women wanted to be heard and not necessarily agreed with. It's the opposite with men, who fight to be right. In a women's group, each woman usually feels that they had a good discussion though no conclusions were reached. In a men's group, they will impatiently cut off conversation to get to the bottom line and make a decision. These are two very different views on the process and purpose of discussion. Without a bottom line, men feel frustrated and question why they even talked in the first place. For women, the talking is the bottom line. They will each make their own decision and an external agreement is not necessary.

I also saw how women can be more vicious to one another than men. They also are more supportive and emotionally in sync with one another. They bond quicker than men. Women are much more in tune with lessons learned from mothers and fathers and recognize that they repeat patterns observed in their childhood homes. Don't forget that it is women who carry on a major proportion of the folk traditions that are passed from one generation to another. Watch how women guard the family photos and memorabilia. It is easier for them to say they are like their mothers than for any man to admit he's like anyone else.

The search for "it" exists in all these discussions, and each person has their own definition. I was lucky to have had such a deeply rewarding experience by hearing all these reflections of life in the raw. "Maybe I did not have your experience, but now I can feel and understand you clearly."

That is what learning "it" is all about.

Learning "It"
From Men

As the Grateful Dead song goes, "What a long, strange trip it's been." Men teaching me about whatever it is to be a man has been a complicated, confusing, and at times disastrous process. From the fifties through the sixties, who and what men were changed dramatically—and so did their messages. In the sixties, Hugh Hefner and his Playboy brand, which objectified women and viewed them as playthings for the suave bachelor, had a drastic effect on the male view of women.

Hefner began his quest to explain what the changing mores of sexual freedom were all about. It was a direct challenge to the established pattern of male sexuality of previous decades. To men of earlier generations, women were either madonnas or whores. Hefner attacked the double standard where men could have as much sex as they wanted without any loss of esteem or character, but women could not. It was a radical idea that women were entitled to the same healthy sexual appetites as men.

I came of age in my teens in the fifties. My young adulthood was spent in the sixties. I liked the change, as women took the pill and enjoyed their new sexual freedom. But the old guard was still in power, much as it is today. There were deep fissures in the culture and in the laws. Both sexes could now have freedom to be with whoever they wanted, as long as it was consensual and you chose someone of the opposite sex. My point is that there were two divergent views of women and of sex. The old guard still judged a woman as "fallen" if she had a lot of sex. The *avant-garde* viewed that as passé. So, some men gave very different advice as to who was a "good woman". This paradigm was played out in dramatic form as men brought home unconventional women to meet the family. This still applies today in more provincial families in rural areas. The urban environment is exactly the opposite: anything goes these days. Even *The New York Times* announces gay couples' engagements on their society page.

Men taught me conflicting and confusing lessons about what my role should be in relation to women. Should I be the provider for the "little lady" at home, or should I be the partner for the modern, educated working woman? Should I take responsibility for finances and make all the decisions, or should this be an equal partnership? Does she need my protection from advances from other men, or should I assume she can handle it on her own without my input? On and on, these very different views crashed into each other. No easy task, this learning "it" thing.

My macho friends took the traditional view of men as needing to be in control to show strength. I found that view rather silly and assumed these guys had small dicks and were overcompensating. I laughed like crazy when I joined the gym and saw the muscle men in the locker room—yep, they were smaller. I tended to take advice more from college guys and older men who had been to college. At that time in my life, I was looking for more philosophical answers rather than those merely passed down without question from family lore and tradition. I ran into difficulty with religious advice as it came more from the latter. Looking back, for example, we now can see the tremendous moral schism the Catholic Church had with its teachings versus the reality of its criminal and abusive behavior. It cost them big time.

I liked the advice of the new male role model of the seventies. Men were now encouraged to be more sensitive and compassionate. "Macho" took a beating as a more genteel man emerged: one who assumed a role in child-rearing, nurturing, and play.

I had just been discharged from the Army during the Vietnam years and, although I never went to active combat, I had received training to do so. The heroic images of WWII and Audie Murphy never did it for me. I threw the grenades, shot my M14, did hand-to-hand combat with knives—but in my soul I was not a killer. Talk about conflict!

In the seventies, I experienced a whole different type of man and for the first time, I related. It was no longer the bunch of guys who went out and got plastered on Friday night, searching for women. The men of the seventies liked their fun, but it was with women in the group—an entirely different mentality.

The James Bond-type role model of the movies had become trite. Now, Cat Stevens, John Denver, and John Lennon were singing about a peaceful, new kind of man with long hair and multi-colored clothing.

My mother swore that I had lost my mind and was more a woman than a man when I wore tight bell bottoms, open shirts, sandals, and jewelry with my flowing, long wavy hair. The men I listened to now spoke highly of women and said that we had much to learn from them. It made sense to me to change my pattern and now look for guidance about "it" from the woman's point of view. I was now cooking, sewing, doing my laundry, ironing, and channeling my aesthetic side. I decorated, planted flowers and did yoga. I felt more balanced; such behavior never hurt my ability to be a self-sufficient male. I started to sip wine instead of gulp it. I acquired two cats, T.C. and Uno. A metamorphosis was happening within me and in the society around me. Men's groups sprang up with sensitivity training, the message being to listen more and talk less. Power was no longer the desired or respected entity (Are you listening, Donald?).

I now listened to men differently as I tended to group them by where their message came from. Was it from traditional marriage and church? Was it from the "old boy" network of "men only" clubs and whiskey? Or was the message more enlightened and educated, roughly referred to as "modern"?

Magazines appeared with articles about living together before marriage—something unheard of in my parents' time. The "new rules" generation who had found their voices in the sixties was changing the social norm … not to say it was all good.

Drugs ruined a major percentage of what that generation could have been. I don't think as a generation they made great parents, either, as they were a bit too narcissistic. But each generation has its strengths and weaknesses. This generation helped women gain their footing more than any other. The suffragettes were an exception rather than the rule in the twenties.

The "It" was changing big time. Although confusing and not without their issues, the roles of men and women were changing rapidly. More and more TV programs dealt with social issues reflecting the changing mores. Archie Bunker made people laugh from his home in Queens while The Jeffersons moved uptown. There would always be the working-class man whose views reflected those like Bunker's, and the women in that realm never burned their bras or marched with Gloria Steinem.

Men were now encouraged to take care of their health. Men's health magazines flourished, and everyone hit the gym. Smoking was no longer fashionable, and smokers were ostracized due to the dangers of passive smoke. Men were now starting to protect the planet as well as their neighborhoods. They were becoming what Hefner had envisioned: more representative of a balanced, integrative male and less of a traditional "manly man". Hefner became a paradox himself—with his pajamas and stupid pipe—a man who still valued image and lounged around with Bunnies. But give him credit: he started something thought-provoking that ultimately benefited both men and women.

Finding "It" is Harder Without a Dad

I can't say I never had one, but I can say I had to make it without one. I met him for the first time when I was three and a half, when he came home from World War II. He was thirty-three with two kids when he was drafted into the Navy and sent to the South Pacific. At age thirty-six he returned home with a ninety-percent disability from the VA due to his war injuries. Within two years, he suffered a major heart attack and had to recover in Florida. He could no longer climb stairs and lost his job as an insurance agent. His VA benefits would end if he entered the workforce and he was prohibited from doing so. My father was a young man with two kids and had limited physical as well as financial abilities. It had to be brutal for him. In the twelve years I knew him, he had three more heart attacks.

My childhood memories of him are mostly comprised of visits to VA hospitals full of men injured in the war. He would tell my mother—with me in the room—not to bring me there. I didn't understand then, but I do now.

When he would return to the house, we all catered to his condition. We would do nothing to frighten or upset him. We had to be quiet all the time—hard to do for a small child. My father napped constantly. I learned how to gently wake him and not startle him. When he felt well enough to go out, we would do errands together. He was good-natured and I know he loved me. Yet, in my efforts to keep him from exerting himself, I became the parent. I took care of him.

If he tried to play ball with me, I could see on his face how little breath he had and how quickly he got tired. I would offer to do something else instead. He tried to coach my baseball little league team, but that required hitting the ball to the infielders for warm-up. I was the catcher, so I took the bat and hit the balls and quickly put on my glove for the return throw, to spare him from getting tired.

One day, he said we were going to a Yankees game, but we had to stop at an apartment building in scary New York City to pick up the tickets. He sent me up to get them. It was my first time, at age ten, in a NYC apartment building. I flew up those steps, found the apartment, and raced back down to the street where my father was waiting. I was so scared that something would happen to me, but there had been no other choice, as my father could not climb stairs. It was part of growing up and overcoming fears, my father said. On the subway en route to the game, he had his third heart attack. I rode alone in the back of the police car that followed the ambulance to the hospital. Trauma had followed trauma. It took me years to return to the subway or enter a hospital.

My father died shortly after my sixteenth birthday, having his last heart attack in the Port Authority, the main bus station for New Jersey and interstate commuters. I had to go through the PA every day for my summer job in the city. I always looked at the fourth step leading down to the subway, because that's where he had collapsed, according to the PA police.

I had learned all I was ever going to learn from my father by the middle of my teens. He valued honesty and hard work. He respected women, and though we never had "the talk", I understood his message that women were to be valued. He had one motto that he repeated often: "If you are going to do something, do it right or don't do it at all."

I did have one very difficult issue with him: he smoked cigarettes, and although he was told by doctors—long before the Surgeon General's warning—to quit, he never did. He said it was one of the few pleasures he had left. My conflict was that his pleasure was going to kill him and therefore be bad for me. It affected his health and contributed to his early demise. I was angry with him for choosing cigarettes over more time with his family.

After he died, I had to find another way to get "it". I watched with envy other fathers and sons walking and talking together. It seemed to me that every other kid had his father there on high school awards night, and that really hurt.

Every kid who has my story has had to adapt and find "it" some other way. Dads are the ones who show you the way, point out the pitfalls, give advice and counsel. They explain how things work in the world. They help you learn how to be a man. They tell you about things you don't know about and keep you from making more mistakes than you would on your own.

I started talking to older men without a conscious idea of what I was doing. It started with making friends with older kids in high school and then in college, where the difference between eighteen and twenty-two is huge. I ate up all the information they gave me, which was not always good. Just because they were older didn't mean their advice was sound. Living through trial and error is common for many. My road to maturity was longer, with lots of detours and a few dead ends.

My mother made one major parenting mistake with me. Shortly after my father died, she told me I had to figure "it" out on my own, because she was a woman. I had to learn how to be a man by myself. True enough, but she should have sought out some form of *in locus patri*—another male family member or a friend. Her life, however, was all about survival. She had limited skills and my father's VA benefits were paltry. She became depressed. Parenting a sixteen-year-old boy was beyond her ability at the time. The "double whammy" for me was losing one parent and then the other, one to death and the other to depression. I was, in effect, on my own. One survives either because of "it" or in spite of "it".

I look back now and can understand why I took off to hitchhike the country, in my search for "it". The people I met on the road became my teachers and helped me replace what I had lost. The men and women who talked to me in the big rigs, the diners, and every place else added to my experience and maturity. Who knows if I would have become as strong as I am had my father lived and shown me "it"? What matters is that you find "it" your way, overcoming the challenges and the barriers. Do whatever you have to do in order to gather the information necessary to become what my mother called a "productive citizen".

I found my way because of a strong, inner drive to have a meaningful life. I had a lot of help. The jazz I listened to at night in my attic calmed my jumbled insides after my father died. Thelonious Monk, Stan Getz, The Modern Jazz Quartet, Cannonball Adderley, Charlie Parker, Ray Charles, and Miles Davis soothed me deep within. Over the years, all forms of music—jazz, folk, rock—all played a role in helping me discover myself. Music can take you away from where you are in the moment. It can uplift your spirits and connect you to feelings never experienced before. It was my first exposure to art. Later, theatre, film, dance, pottery, and other art forms followed suit in my progress toward adulthood.

The creative process is the development of "it". The information comes into the self and then some internal magic happens and out come words, songs, paintings, dances—or maybe nothing at all. Some of "it" can just stay inside a person, the result yet to be determined.

Add it all up and I can say that I have loved the journey, however varied, unpredictable, and challenging. I wouldn't change my experience for anything.

My First Teachers

Who were your teachers? The ones who changed you? Made you think differently, deeper. Made you more aware. Taught you lessons in consequences.

My first teacher who changed me was Miss O'Malley. She was a true spinster who dedicated herself to teaching: tall, thin, horn-rimmed glasses and completely covered from neck to toe. Prim and proper, she wore what we called clodhoppers—shoes with large, square heels that clunked along the floor. Think of Spencer Tracy's movies: the courthouse women all wore them.

I was in Miss O'Malley's seventh grade geography class. She was exceptionally polite and addressed the rowdy bunch of hormone-crazed teenagers as "Mr." and "Miss". She demanded proper sitting positions in class: no slouching, no arms folded. "Sit up and pay attention!" The magic was that she controlled a class that had sent more people to the principal's office than any other—but she got 100% obedience. Everyone wanted her approval, which was warm and sincere. You earned her respect by learning and participating in class.

I never heard Jimmy Melloni speak in class, except in Miss O'Malley's. When I asked him why he spoke there and nowhere else, he said, "Everywhere else in this school I am an asshole or a J. D. (juvenile delinquent), but here I am Mr. Melloni—treat me good and I return the favor."

When class was over, no one rushed for the door. You stood up by your seat and row one left in single file, followed by row two and so on. If someone did talk while Miss O'Malley was speaking, she would just stop and look at the rude speaker. The class would grow quiet, exposing the person to further rebuke. Miss O'Malley never said anything mean or angry, never called anyone a name. It was magical. She was all about respect, dignity, and politeness. She made geography interesting and to this day I know where countries are on the map, or at least where they used to be. But the primary lesson Miss O'Malley taught me was to give respect first and it will come back to you. Thank you, Miss O.

Howie Wolf was a high school football coach who saw me playing baseball and came up to me and said, "Do you want to learn to throw a pass?" I told him I could already throw a pass. He said, "Not in the street, but as quarterback on the team, with real pressure all around you."

I had never thought about it as my love was baseball. Coach Wolf volunteered to coach me if I promised to try out for the J. V. team the following year. I agreed, and Howie Wolf worked with me on proper grip, arm angle, foot coordination and how to read speed in order to lead a moving target. He put up targets for me to hit, getting farther away each time I hit one. He showed he believed in me, and I worked harder for him than anyone else who had ever coached me. I wound up starting for the high school JV football team and we had the first winning season ever. He bought me the team jacket after the season was over. You never know what you are capable of, until someone believes in you and you ask more of yourself. That's always a good thing.

Mr. Miller was a very short man and made self-deprecating jokes as he stood in front of the class. "Everyone can see me, right?" He told us that in his class you can't fake it. Either your answer was right, or it was not. No interpretations. If he was wrong, you could also prove him wrong. He added, "Try to do that—it will keep me on my toes, and I could use a few inches."

I loved the guy. I learned so much from him that by the time I was struggling in college with my BA requirements, I would take electives in math just to keep up my GPA. Who ever thought math could be fun? Two tens for a five was never going to get me.

Teachers can be anywhere. James was his name. He had a vinyl record shop on 42nd Street in New York City. I was sixteen and passed it every day on my way to work my summer job in the city. The front portion of the store sold girlie magazines and it was a bit intimidating, as I didn't even know if I was allowed in. In typical adolescent fashion, when I summoned up the courage to go inside, I walked up directly to him and told him that I was there only for the records. James laughed. "Not interested in girls?" he said. I did not know what to say, and he kept laughing. "So, you want a record?" he finally asked. "Yes, sir," I replied. "Well, go pick one out and show me what you got," he said.

As it turned out, I picked out "Ray Charles, Live at Newport". "Good choice," James said when I showed him. "You know Ray Charles?" "No, but the picture on the cover looks great," I said.

The following week I returned. "Back again?" James said. I told him the album was great and that I had never heard that kind of sound before.

James became my mentor as he pointed me to the blues and soul section. He told me about Basin St East and the 5 Spot, Village Gate, Birdland, The Metropole and the Village Vanguard. I started going to these NY clubs where I could hear these artists live. Then, it was on to jazz. I embarked on a passion that still exists today.

Being a teenager, I didn't want to be seen coming out of a girlie mag store with a brown paper bag. I would proudly carry my un-covered album out of the store and not worry if my neighborhood people passing by on their way to the Port Authority saw me. James even gave me a free album after I thanked him for showing me a new world.

Larry was a long-hauler. He had a big rig and rode coast to coast. I was hitching at the time to San Francisco. He picked me up outside Pittsburgh and we talked for a while. He realized how young and green I was and asked me what I had in my knapsack. I told him I had some basic toiletries and a change of clothes. We went through Ohio and stopped at a Union 76, a huge truck stop, which included a large merchandise store. Larry said I needed more basics: a poncho, some toilet paper, and a sewing kit. A flashlight would be good, and a small knife and fork set, and some Band-Aids—things that had never crossed my mind.

We talked about the road and how it was better to hitch from gas stations and diners as you can talk to people before you get into their cars or trucks. He told me to never hitch on an open highway and never on the road in the rain. He advised me to get my last ride before the sun went down and know exactly where and when I'd be getting out. There was nothing worse than being dropped in the middle of nowhere at night.

Larry told me to talk to waitresses, because they knew everything about people and travel. What he said was simple, direct, and right on the button. What I learned from Larry was never taught in school. He also advised me to get a good detailed map with motels and restaurants listed. This was long before cell phones and Siri. He also told me to get a thermos, as I would always need water—and "don't forget the aspirin!" By the end of his lesson, I needed a bigger knapsack.

Mr. Baldwin gave me advice that saved my life. He was my supervisor at the Department of Social Services on East 5th Street in New York's Lower East Side. He helped me navigate the tenements with good solid information about what to expect in dealing with indigent people including blacks, Hispanics, the elderly, and single mothers. We formed a warm and close relationship. I would say he even parented me. Mr. Baldwin was black, and he was always on the lookout for "attitude" among young white social workers. He saw lots of prejudice out of those who wanted to "stop the cheaters". Mr. Baldwin and I talked long and hard about the "deserving" and "undeserving" poor, which the government differentiated by their programs. Deserving poor received benefits, undeserving poor got handouts. This is still going on today in congressional debates.

I learned how to ask personal questions that were aimed at helping and not just prying. Mr. Baldwin was a deeply caring man. When I got my draft notice during the build-up to Vietnam, I was completely shattered. I was against the war and certainly did not want to die, especially as a soldier. He felt my fears. He put his arm around me and said, "Do you know there is Social Work in the Army? They have counseling and social services, so if you get the chance, tell them you are a social worker with a college degree."

On my third day in the Army, the sergeant in charge asked the assembled five hundred privates if "anyone has a degree in Psychology and can prove it". Mr. Baldwin's words had come true and I put up my hand. Long story short, I spent two years being trained and supervised in a psych clinic in Heidelberg, Germany, and not in the rice paddies of Vietnam. On my return, Columbia University gave me a scholarship for their MSW program. Once I graduated, I went on to get my ACSW, LCSW and Certificate and License in Family Therapy. How's that for good advice? Love you, Mr. Baldwin—you certainly showed "it" to me.

Selling "It" with Falcon Eddie

I was dirt poor during my college years and had to work full time to support myself. I was living in an apartment and had the usual bills: rent, gas, electric, telephone, and food. I had a buddy living with me as he had just broken up a bad relationship and wasn't flying high, either. He contributed his share.

My job began at 4am at UPS, where I cleaned the bathrooms, scrubbed the grease off the floor after the trucks pulled out, and kept the locker room clean. My shift was over at noon, and then I rode my motorcycle to college as I could not afford a car. It was not fun in the rain.

I would return home about 6pm and study until bedtime at ten. Then it was up at 3:20am and off to work. If you want a lesson in endurance, this would be it. I was tired all the time.

I still did not make enough money to cover all my expenses, so I had a Saturday job from 9am to 2pm. I had answered an ad for a cash-only opportunity to work with a man who would pick me up and drive me home. So far so good. The job involved some training and then I would be working on my own. Doing what? Selling bibles, door to door.

This man Eddie drove a Ford Falcon—not a high-end vehicle by a long shot. He offered a one-day training class and then he would pick you up the next Saturday at 8am sharp. The training was to learn about this fancy bible he was selling out of the back of the Falcon. Being Jewish didn't faze him a bit. If anyone asked, I was a Catholic college student, going to Seton Hall and trying to lower my parents' costs.

Ethics never entered the conversation. He would say, "Look, it's a beautiful book with gilded edges and it has a section where you write down your family tree and pass it on, one generation to another." I had to learn about the imprimatur and the different sections. It was a large, quality book. Eddie highlighted all its selling points.

On our first Saturday, three other salesmen and myself piled into the Falcon and drove to Elizabeth, New Jersey—a hardscrabble, working-class town with a lot of Catholic churches. We didn't stop at the police station to get our permit to sell. Eddie said he had them. If anyone questioned us, we were to tell them the boss will be back in the afternoon and he would answer any questions and show the permits.

The book sold for twenty-five dollars, but there was a catch: if you paid one dollar today, Eddie would give you the bible and then return each week and collect another buck. A person had the option to pay it off sooner. "Dollar down, dollar a week, great deal, and we trust you" was the sales pitch. For a down payment sale, I earned six dollars. If they paid full price that day, I got twelve.

"Falcon Eddie" really did give people the book for one dollar. "It's a goddamn bible!" he would say to us. "These Catholics would feel guilty stealing a bible—it would create bad juju." No matter the question, Eddie had an answer.

For me, this job was a slow-grinding, ethical process of guilt versus reward. On one hand, the book itself was quality and the customers could choose to buy it or not. I thought they were getting a good deal. But why all the lying? Eddie would say, "They don't want some Jewish kid from Weehawken selling them their bible. They want a good Catholic kid who needs money to help his parents with college costs." I did not like lying, but the cash was good. Isn't that what every drug dealer says? "They want it, and I am only the supplier."

We did this for about six weeks, and then the wheels came off. I pushed the wrong doorbell—one that belonged to one of the elders of a local Catholic church. His first question was, "Does the Monsignor know you are selling these, as we sell our own bibles to our congregation." I gave him my standard reply: "My boss will answer all your questions."

The man called the police and the Church. The cops came and put me in the squad car before they drove around and picked up the other salesmen. We went down to the station to sort it all out. It turned out this wasn't the first time that "Falcon Eddie" had caught the attention of the authorities. They had numerous complaints on file of his coming by at odd hours to collect his dollar. He had even propositioned single mothers, saying there were "other ways" to pay off the bible. *Jeez!*

The cops weren't interested in us—they dropped us off at our pick-up spot and waited for the Falcon. When Eddie drove up, they confiscated the bibles and issued him a summons for soliciting without a license. "No problem," Eddie told us. "Next week we'll go to Linden or Rahway."

We all quit. It was one thing to work for Falcon Eddie when we did not know what was going on, and another when we did. Some people got "it" for only a dollar, as he was banned from returning to Elizabeth. For me, my days of being a Catholic student from Seton Hall were over.

It Was the Best of Times

I remember living in Greenwich Village during the best of times: the end of the Beatnik era and the beginning of the music and cultural explosion of the sixties. The scene was everywhere, from Warhol in the East Village to Bill Graham and the Fillmore. The Village Voice was at its peak, the underground film world was exploding, and avant-garde theater was creative and fresh. Gloria Steinem and Betty Friedan were leading the Women's Movement. Gays were taking a stand against the police in the Stonewall uprising. The streets were festive with be-ins and omnipresent, spontaneous events. LSD and other mind-expanding drugs were a centerpiece of the counterculture. The Pill liberated women. The Beatles dominated the music scene with "Sgt. Pepper" and "Magical Mystery Tour". Woodstock and the Golden State's Wild West festival were the largest such gatherings to date. Protesters flooded the streets to protest the war in Vietnam. It seemed that the young were going to change the staid culture of America.

But the pushback began. The Rockefeller drug laws started putting small-time, soft drug users away for ungodly amounts of time. Police became more armed and violent following the Black Panther Movement, and then there was the death of the hippie movement with the violent, bloody Hell's Angels massacre at the Stones concert at Altamont. Rock stars like Janis Joplin, Jimi Hendrix, and Jim Morrison were overdosing and the flowers with their messages of love and peace were replaced with the nihilistic punk scene in places like CBGB's. The beautiful people turned ugly as I witnessed my friends who had partied in the sixties dying in the seventies. I was thirty-five, single, and I knew that if I continued living the night scene, I would be joining them.

It was the classic "too much of a good thing". So, I bit the bullet and bought a five-bedroom house in the suburbs that cost eleven of the twelve thousand dollars I had to my name. That was me: if you believe in yourself, go all in. It ended up being a fantastic decision for me, and it's still paying off forty years later.

I had my cats and my plants, plus I kept the apartment in the Village so I wouldn't go "cold turkey". It was not an easy adjustment: I had never lived in a house and I was a total stranger to suburban life. I stood out, for sure. I scared the hell out of the little Welcome Wagon lady who stopped by with gifts. In my city-mind, no one gave you anything for free that didn't have a hook in it. The poor woman was completely flustered when I kept asking her who she was and why she wanted to give me stuff.

The move out of the city saved me, as I started to go to bed before 2am. I worked in an outpatient psychiatric clinic during the day. I am not saying the suburbs are the way to go; I am just saying that suburban life broke me away from the upside-down world of living at night and not relating to the day (Ask any musician). I was one of the lucky ones, to be there in the Village, in the middle of everything for all those years, and then to survive and keep my health and mind intact. It is not the usual story. To have been part of the uprising, to have witnessed a cultural revolution, to have heard some of the best music ever, and to be alive fifty years later to talk and write about it, feels kind of special. "It" brought me to the Village, and "it" told me when it was time to leave.

Marty and Sweetface

When I lived in Greenwich Village, I loved shooting pool. My love for billiards had begun long before, when I took over my grandmother's apartment after she and Pop-Pop retired to Florida. I was twenty and going to college while I also worked very low-level jobs.

The first thing I did when I moved in was to remove the top of the dining room table from the legs. The top was in two halves, with a leaf in the middle. I bought a used, French Provincial pool table with a slate top and after nearly killing myself getting it upstairs, I placed Nanny's tabletop over it. I covered it so my mother wouldn't go out of her mind seeing what I had done to Nanny's table.

The fifteen second tabletop removal maneuver revealed a blue felt pool table, right there in the dining room. I practiced between studies and work. I became skilled enough to make some extra cash later, when I hitchhiked across the country. I made money in bars and pool halls from Fayetteville to Tucson, and Mobile to Bozeman.

In the Village, around the corner from me, was the Greenwich Tavern. It used to be called the International and it was on Greenwich Street, a tiny bar with a pool table. There were many such bars in the Village in those days, catering to the local working class such as delivery men, plumbers, electricians, and business people. At night, these establishments morphed into places that drew their own specific crowd. Julius on Tenth Street, for example, served a great hamburger and people flocked there during the day. At night, it catered to an older, gay male crowd. The younger gays were on Christopher Street at the Stonewall or Ty's.

The Greenwich Tavern was just a tavern until it slowly became a gay women's bar. I used to go there in the afternoon to shoot pool. As it happened, I hadn't noticed the change in clientele when I went there one evening.

A very large woman greeted me in the doorway. "Where the fuck do you think you're going?" she asked. "Inside," I replied calmly. "Not for you, Sweetface," she replied.

The woman had very short, parted hair and wore a big pair of jeans and a t-shirt with the sleeves rolled, reminiscent of the Marlon Brando-type bikers of the fifties. She also wore thick, studded leather wristbands and around her neck hung a gold name plate that read "Marty". I guessed her to be close to two hundred pounds, not the sort of person you ignore or walk past.

I stepped back. "Marty?" I said. "I live around the corner on Eleventh Street and I have been shooting pool in this joint for years. Does it still have a pool table?"

"Yep," came her terse reply.

"Well then, with your permission, I would like to shoot some pool."

She just laughed. "Listen, Sweetface, the place has changed, and 'my' people are in there, so stick to pool and leave everyone else alone." With that, she stepped aside, and I went in.

The place was mostly the same—only the patrons had changed. Everyone looked me up and down as I walked in. "Is Marty outside?" one woman asked me. "Yes, I had the pleasure," I told her. "Don't mind her," the woman said. "She thinks she runs the place—she's just a bad bull." After our initial encounter, Marty and I were now on much friendlier terms. "I hear you shoot a good game," she said to me. "I get by," I replied.

The women in the place shot pool well. There was a sign announcing a tournament that would begin at the Greenwich Tavern—the West Village championship was then to be played over at a gay women's bar on Greenwich Avenue for the final round. I signed up.

The women kidded with one another and "broke balls", as it is in most gay circles. Comments can go from hysterically funny to cutting. Getting your ass grabbed was a sign of acceptance. Who knew? The spectrum of people in the bar was like everywhere else, from very attractive and "feminine-looking", to those more like Marty:

rough, no makeup, with a strong authority stance and a fierce command of street language. I was there for the pool, and because I shot well, I earned their respect and made some friends. After shooting, I would sit with the girls and have some beers. Marty dominated the action in the bar. She loved busting my chops.

The tournament began and I did very well. Marty became a loud fan of my game. "Too bad you are a guy, or I could sweep you up," she said to me one night after too many beers. I won the tournament and was now representing the Greenwich at the finals. It was very odd, and not everyone was happy with a guy representing a gay woman's bar. Marty shouted down the dissenters: "He beat every one of you bitches, so shut the fuck up!"

I hadn't seen Marty for a week and that was unusual. When I went to the finals on Greenwich Avenue, sure enough, there was Marty, working the door. She was now an official bouncer. When I approached, she gave me a strong shot in the arm. "Jeezus, Marty! I may need that arm someday." "Good luck, Sweetface, but this place is different—you'll see," she said, as she opened the door for me.

It was much bigger than the Greenwich and the women were scantily clad. Some looked very sexy. The "bulls" ran the place, and there was a lot of "attitude". There was only one other guy in the tournament. He knew the rules: "Hands off".

After three rounds of finals over a two-week period, I made it into the final round. Marty was my biggest supporter. "My money's on Sweetface!" she bellowed from the front door. Do you have any idea how awkward it was to be called "Sweetface" in that environment?

There was this absolutely beautiful woman with high cheek bones playing in the tournament. She wore tight jeans and some sort of revealing top each night. The night bartender was her lover, a woman more like Marty. It was now down to four remaining players and I was paired against her. Like every town with a home-field advantage, the bar crowd was for her. She upped her game one more level: for our match, she wore a loose, low-cut blouse, and each time she leaned over the table to shoot, her breasts were exposed. She would curl her lips into the greatest smile every time she shot, making it clear to the crowd that she knew what she was doing. It was the oldest trick in the book: try to make your opponent lose their concentration.

"Marty," I said to my friend, "that's just plain wrong." All the girls in the bar loved it, of course. The comments flew: "Nice set—wish I had 'em!"; "How's that, Sweetface?"; "Chalk those nipples, girl!" and "Titties rule!" It was hard not to look. I was still a guy, after all.

"It" had worked—my concentration was compromised. I walked away from the table to gather myself. I grumbled out loud to no one: "I'm a guy, not just a pool player. This is cheating."

Then, I heard the perfect response for someone in my situation: "Take your dick out!" came the shout from the door.

The place went crazy. Despite the chants, hoots and hollers, I chose to keep it zipped. When it was my turn, my opponent was not in my view and my concentration returned to the task at hand. I won the damned thing, and Marty gave me a crushing hug, nearly lifting me off the floor. She had a friend draw a perfect set of naked breasts on a white t-shirt with the words "The Winner" underneath.

I wore the shirt at the Greenwich and then I wore it to the Upper West Side Tournament. You had to picture Marty and I making an unforgettable entrance at Tap-a Keg, a Columbus Avenue straight bar. Marty, acting like she was the barker outside the circus tent, bounces in, points to me and shouts, "I got your Fucking-A, West Village Tournament Champ right here! Say hello to Sweetface!"

Midwest Surprise

In the early seventies, I had a job cooking hamburgers at the Corner Bistro, a noted Greenwich Village bar and local hangout. It was a friendly place that also attracted tourists, mainly in the late afternoon and evenings. It was a busy job, as there was a back room with nine tables and the front part of the bar had three more. I had to take orders as well as cook the burgers and fries *and* get drinks from the bar.

During the lulls, I would talk to the clientele, the local regulars. There was one woman who came in about three times per week, around two in the afternoon, always by herself. She sat at a small table in the corner. Her name was Margaret and she was a plain-looking woman, about 5' 9". She wore long, flowing dresses, big horn-rimmed glasses and her hair was pulled back tightly in a ponytail.

Margaret lived in the neighborhood in an upstairs apartment.

She would order the ham and cheese sandwich and a beer. When we talked, she told me she had recently moved from Minnesota with some inheritance money and planned to start a business.

Margaret was looking for a small storefront as she wanted to open a sewing shop. It matched her quiet, provincial appearance. None of the men in the bar ever hit on her—she had that semi-proper vibe. After a few weeks, she found a tiny storefront in the neighborhood.

She and I became friends and occasionally had dinner or coffee together. I never considered it dating. One day, she told me she was also a writer. She wrote at night. "Anything I might have read?" I asked. "Oh, no" she replied. She only wrote short stories. Her day job was the sewing shop and she didn't want to work a lot of hours, saying the shop was her way to show the family back home that she had achieved her goal of starting a business.

When the guys would ask me about her, I told them she was a small-town girl from the Midwest who was quietly finding her way in the Big City. She made sure to keep her lunch break at the Bistro. This pattern went on for over a year.

I had the sense that she was a little too quiet about her personal life, as I didn't hear about friends or lovers. She had this invisible wall around her that suggested "Private". She was very quick-witted and funny as we talked politics and "the Village". She had graduated from Minnesota with a degree in Literature and would laugh as the only job to be had with that degree was to stand on a soap box and recite.

One afternoon, she told me to stop by after work, as she was trying out pastry-making and needed a "guinea pig". I had known her for about a year and a half and had never seen her apartment. No one had. After work, I stopped by. It was a typical NYC apartment, but not as "frilly" as other NY women's apartments. Since she owned a sew shop, I had expected to see lots of hand-made stuff. I was wrong: her place was minimalist, with modern art designs.

We sat at her kitchen table as she served some outstanding German nut pastries. I complimented her highly when she said it was her family recipe and she was just starting to try to make them.

Next to the table was a pile of small books. They looked like old-time, detective story books. As I looked closer, the titles surprised me: *She's Gotta Have It, Lonely Night Adventures, Insatiable* … She said nothing but watched me closely as I looked at them. I picked one up and leafed through it. It used explicit sexual language, in an old-time form. Not real, cutting-edge pornography, but these books definitely would be sold on the "separate" table. "You like to read these?" I asked. She paused, smiled, and with a tad of embarrassment admitted, "I write them."

So, Miss Minnesota, the prim and proper small business sewing shop owner, writes pornos. She had about fifteen published and said she was now working on a cable tv show on a public access channel that didn't censor. I told her that I had a Thursday night cable tv show on the same channel called "Village Neighborhood Television" where I did street interviews on topics of the day, mainly from Washington Square Park. I used NYU's editing facilities. Margaret said that some shop owner on 4th Street wanted her to do an "advice" show and sell "products". She would not be doing any editing as they would do the show live. They were working out the details.

Over the next few months, Margaret showed interest in my show and helped me with the topics of the week. She soon announced that her show would air late-night next on Tuesdays and Fridays. She didn't say much more about it, only that it would be one of the "new" shows for public cable.

I missed her first two shows, but she said it got a big audience the second night. It was called "Late Night with Miss Vanessa".

"Catchy title," I told her.

"Just watch it," she replied.

I tuned in to see "Miss Vanessa" dressed in a black leather, low-cut outfit with mesh stockings. She wore a long, black wig and had dark eye makeup, with black lipstick, Gothlike. She sat on a couch with a phone: it was a call-in show for NY's late-night fringe. This was brand new, even for New York! It was a downtown version of uptown's peep shows.

"Miss Vanessa" would answer the callers' questions, which were hyper-personal and formulated for shock value. She was nonplussed as she answered questions about every orifice on the human body and what you could do to it. Then, she would pause and sell her sex toy products, including flavored lubes as well as whips, chains, handcuffs, dildos, and gags. There were strange-looking leather combos as well as different types of restraints. The whole product list from the new W 4th Street sex shop was hers to use. The show became the rage of cable. It was the forerunner of many shows of this type that soon found their way onto the airwaves.

Margaret wanted her privacy, and I never told anyone that "Miss Minnesota Horn-Rims Sewing Shop Owner" was the one and only "Miss Vanessa". The old adage, "Don't judge a book by its cover", goes for the author as well.

"It" Lives in Kitchen Conversations

What is it about the kitchen that spurs so many intimate and philosophical conversations? Do you think it's the universality of food that makes people reveal their secrets while cooking? I am not only talking about the meal itself, where everyone sits around the table and talks. I am speaking of the one that takes place during food preparation, while vegetables are being washed, sliced, and diced, or while the meat is marinating and the potatoes are being peeled.

If you like to cook like I do, there is a ritual that cooks go through when they prepare a meal. From the selection of pots and pans, to the utensils and spices used, it is almost a dance with familiar steps. Most cooks will tell you that having more than one cook in a kitchen is an unwanted crowd, but having helpers is fine.

I think most people cook from their family recipes first, and then they add, adjust, and modify to suit their tastes. But starting with the basic family recipe, I believe, is what starts the tongue wagging.

Who does not remember the food of their childhood, who made it, and what it smelled like? Those memories and stories can be told for generations as new helpers are brought into the kitchen. Nanny would tell me about old Germany and her iron pots and huge oven. She would recount her days from going with her mother to the markets in the morning to buy the meat and vegetables for the meal and the fruits she might use to make the pie for dessert. She would tell me stories about her demanding father and her troubled sister, who always had to be told to not start fights at the table.

I remember my mother talking about Nanny whenever I helped her in the kitchen. My mother's stories centered around her own scrutiny over the selection of foods at the market. I remember a story about her demanding that the butcher give her a prime cut of meat: she had specific instructions about how much fat was to be left. She would pick each string bean separately by first inspecting it—same for the carrots and cucumbers and especially the fruits. When we finally got back to the kitchen, she would ask if I watched carefully how she did things, because not only was it the "right" way, but it was the only way.

I used to listen to my mother instructing my older sister not only about the ways of the kitchen, but the ways of life. She would tell my sister that if she wanted to keep a man, she had to learn how to make him a good meal and be a good wife in the bedroom. I was young and didn't understand what the bedroom had to do with him being happy.

I overheard conversations in the homes where my mother

visited. She had an Italian friend, Lola, who took extreme pride in her meal preparation and she even gave advice to my mother as well. I watched her flit from pan to pan as she cut the tomatoes and grilled the garlic and added the spices. I was in awe as she cut the onions and peppers precisely and added them to the mysterious pot that had all the red gravy. She would say, "Italian men are very fussy and if you don't make the pasta and gravy like their mothers did, it will cause a problem."

The other women of Lola's extended family were always in the kitchen, talking about their marriages, their children, and their relatives. The conversations were loud and passionate. I heard some words about other women from them that I did not understand, but they always said it with arms and hands waving in the air. Opera was always playing in the background, and at times they would all stop talking and start singing, with arms over heads and cupped hands pointing skyward.

The aromas filled the kitchen and the men would arrive home from work and come into the kitchen to get a little taste, only to be instantly banished. This was hallowed ground to these women, and men did not belong. Lola always told my mother, "If men want to cook, they should open a restaurant!"

I heard so many marvelous stories about the history of their family. Every family tells these stories. There is always a near-crazy aunt whom no one can understand. There is always a philandering male whom everyone loves and hates at the same time.

When we went to my father's family home for kitchen talk it was almost the same, but men were more strictly forbidden to enter. This was serious turf to my Jewish aunts. They would announce when the kitchen was open for helpers to carry the food to the dining room. The food never smelled as good in their kitchen, and that was borne out at the table as well. They boiled the potatoes and over-cooked the veggies. The Italians usually baked or sautéed the potatoes and they added spices. But I was told by my mother to say nothing and only open my mouth to eat.

Now that I have been cooking for years, I enjoy having people in the kitchen, although I am a serious controller of timing and what should go next and on and on, as the apple does not fall far from the tree. Once those hierarchical lines are established, I also love to use the time for conversation about people, places, and things. I love to talk about the food of other countries and compare one style of cuisine to another. Cooking Moroccan will always elicit stories of being in the Medina, in Marrakech. Making Thai food always brings out conversations of elephants or monks. Mexican food night evokes stories about the fabulous cuisine of Mexico City, or me trying to beat the flavor of the local Mexican taco guy.

I believe food and preparation bring out life stories that are passed on from one generation to the next, as it does with women doing the communal laundry. Ever witness that phenomenon? It crosses all cultures. As women gather, either by the river or at the laundromat, they tell their stories and pass them along. There is something magical about coming home with clean laundry: its smell and its warmth make everyone feel good. It is the same with a meal that has been traditionally prepared, with rituals from family history, spiced with good family stories and served with love. Dig in, everyone. "It" is being served.

Look In, Not Out

Look in, not out. Sounds easy, but what does it mean? We live in this dichotomy world of the West and the East. Generally, in the West, it's all about consuming: more, bigger, better. Discard the semi-new for the newer. Move up the proverbial ladder. The pressure is relentless, and we see the casualties from it every day—people reacting to anxiety and stress, needing detox and rehab; people drinking too much in order to cope, or "relax" as they call it, after a brutal day, week, or month. Meanwhile, they consume fast food because of their hectic pace, wolfing down processed food as they drive, further wrecking their health.

No matter how much information is available, people continue the Western pursuit of "success": The amount of medication taken in order to meet these goals is staggering, but that is the capitalist way: there will always be someone to sell you something for the problem you now have, even if they sold you the problem in the first place. Doesn't it seem like the side effects they tell you about on TV should make you *not* want to take the drug? But if you do, they will have something else to sell you as a remedy.

The new solution is to buy a super-expensive condo in a building that has everything at your fingertips, so you don't ever have to leave the building. *That's* progress? What ever happened to fresh air, a brisk walk, or an apple? I am not saying our active culture doesn't encourage you to ride a bike or go mountain climbing—but don't forget you need the "best bike and equipment".

The West is reliant on television and internet as the selling media. Look at the money spent to sell you a car or an image. For women, it is over the top in the number of products they are told they need. The one thing all these ads have in common is the message of how you will "look" wearing, buying, or riding in the product. It is about endless consumption. The ad men will tell you it is their way of getting better and improving. But when does it stop? When do you ever have enough, if having "it" is what you want?

Let's take a moment to go East, which also has its own "West", as Japan, Korea, and China are just about as "West" as we are. Traditional East is my focus here, where possessions are not needed nor wanted. People in the East seek an inner connectedness where one is in harmony with the natural universe. Their belief is that what one is searching for is already inside them and therefore their task to seek it out. Monks take vows of poverty and rely on others to provide for them, though they do grow their own food. They all wear the same clothing to reduce comparison and competition. The spiritual self is the ultimate pleasure. The power of the concentration released by these believers is something to behold. Once they have obtained "it", they can alter their own body temperatures or even change the temperature of a room. Thought power is centered and requires a journey to find "it". There are likely capitalists right now who are trying to figure out what "it" is so they can bottle it and sell it. Such was the attempt in the 19th century when charlatans peddled "magic elixirs" along the American frontier. What the monks have can't be bottled and sold.

You have to give the West credit for trying, however. There isn't a town in America now that doesn't have a yoga or Pilates class. Gyms are everywhere, pushing cycling, wall climbing, weightlifting, cross-training, swimming—and don't forget to purchase those supplements!

In the East, there are no monk gyms: they don't need them! They never let themselves fall into conditions of "disrepair". Their lives are not about consumption and the resulting debilitating stress.

I know one man who lives in both worlds. He is an extremely peaceful, moral man who leads a spiritually and financially successful life and gives back from his success. He calls himself a "Bu-Jew". A conservative Jew who made it on Wall Street, then left the market environs for ethical reasons and became a Buddhist. He now owns a wealth alignment center that only invests people's money in companies that are providing "the good", meaning companies that are making something that does no harm or helps promote a feeling of well-being.

One such company I observed—nothing to do with my

friend—was a tourist company in Southeast Asia that took people from the streets and trained them to work in their hotels and restaurants, giving them marketable skills. The workers had to send their children to one of the company's highly competent, free schools. The hotels and restaurants they used had to offer decent wages and benefits. Products made by employees were sold on-site. In summary, they took people off the streets where they were maltreated and at risk and gave them a marketable skill set, employing them while their children received free educations. All this was funded by tourists who reaped the benefits of well-staffed, expertly run hotels. Once the tourists saw the system in action, they could voluntarily help support it if they wanted—a win-win situation all around.

My friend supports institutions like this. There are good businesses in America who are trying to do the right thing while they make a profit. My friend seeks them out and holds seminars for the general public, where information is passed on. He has a huge list of speakers who also live in the world of ethical balance. The "it" here takes years and years. You just don't learn this stuff overnight. But you can want to, and I believe it is necessary in the USA, if we are going to save ourselves from our unethical "profit at any cost" model. It's only a few at the top, in the big-profit companies, who make the money and make sure it never trickles down.

It seems a zillion years ago that Jimmy Stewart told us to do the right thing because it was the right thing to do. When it was done for everyone, no one got hurt. The monks don't hurt anyone by looking inside and writing about it. The gurus and lamas are trying to stem the imbalance by teaching how to find peace. It certainly won't be found with nuclear weapons.

If you want to see how cultures operate in harmony within their environments, study the indigenous populations of the world. They make everything from what they have and use it expertly: food and clothing from animals; housing from trees and rocks; medicine from plants. They make no plastic or chemical preservatives. Their leftovers are either eaten by the animals or used for other purposes. There is a balance to life and a seamless circle of existence.

Then came the conquerors, who systematically eliminated them from their environments. The indigenous were labeled "savages" who needed "saving". Their salvation was their demise. For example, only small pockets of pure Native American culture remain. How sad that the "improved" society we imposed on them has brought us to a crisis in the survival of the planet. Some deny that temperatures and oceans are rising. Why? Power. More control means more profit. Lack of community has helped global warming spin out of control. We face uncertain times in leadership crisis. I, for one, want the old-fashioned philosophy of Jimmy Stewart to be our guide. If we do "it" for the right reason, which means it does no harm and benefits all, then all the people, animals, fish, birds, and plants will survive.

You Find "It" Where You Find It

As you can see, "it" is anywhere, anytime. The beauty is that sometimes you never see it coming, because you were doing something else at the time. Here's an example:

To try to stay in shape, I used to run. I did it for forty years, which included three knee operations (I am very stubborn). Finally, there was no cartilage left and I had to stop. But when I was running, I found I could run farther each week as my legs got stronger and my endurance increased. The best runs were along the beach in East Hampton, early in the morning with the sun just up and the calm breeze blowing along the water's edge.

I was doing my usual pace and I decided to push it up a bit. I was surprised that I was not winded, so I increased it a bit more. Still not feeling tired, I kept going faster. After five minutes I notched it up to full speed—and then "it" happened. I absolutely did not feel my legs under me as I raced along the beach effortlessly. I was not winded at all as I continued this marvelous feeling of being bodyless. "It" was my first experience of the "runner's high", where the brain produces those wonderful alpha waves and a total feeling of contentment overtakes you.

A woman I knew from the city was coincidentally on the beach, watching me run. When I finished and was sitting on my towel, she came over and said to me, "That was the most beautiful run I ever saw. You looked like a racehorse with your hair flowing in the wind and how effortless it looked. It took my breath away." How's that for a double-high?

I learned more about the "runner's high" when I started running with others. They said it usually kicks in about twenty-five minutes into the run if your pace is fast enough. You must be in shape for it to occur, and you can't overdo it early on as it's a gradual build-up. It was my first natural high. "It" was why I kept going back to the operating table to fix my knees so I could continue to experience that feeling of well-being and happiness without having to smoke anything or pop some sort of pill.

Others have told me about other forms of exercise that give them this same feeling. I have known many guys who get their good feelings from an enervated game of basketball, where they are completely soaked when done. Battle beaten and bruised, they love the entire experience. I knew a guy who hung a 75 lb. heavy bag in his basement. He put on some boxing gloves and threw one punch after another until he could no longer feel his hands. He said the feeling that comes after is as good as sex—I don't know about that one, but I'll take his word for it.

A woman in my building swims the Olympic-size pool like she has a motor. Back and forth she darts through the water, flipping her feet against the wall to propel herself back across the pool. She describes the experience as "losing herself". She said that she never felt that good anywhere else.

There are four guys who play handball against the wall at 3rd Street and Sixth Avenue in the Village. They wear sweat bands around their heads and fingerless leather gloves while they play four or five intense games until they are drained. To them, the score is irrelevant. What matters is that they get the feeling of calm that follows.

In the morning, I often meet a man who is taking his racing bike off the elevator for his twenty-mile "run". He likes to go uphill first, so that when he returns he can race to his finish line downhill. He describes "it" the same way as the others: "After a while, you feel like you are not sitting or making the bike go, as it seems to go by itself."

The martial arts teachers talk about getting into a "zone" with their art. The feeling is that same sensation that others describe. The body seems to know how to make us feel good—we just need to channel it through our own methods. The ending result will be "it".

"It" is Big in the Therapist's Office

After fifty years of practice, I guess you could imagine that I have heard just about all of "it". With the telling of each person's life history, out comes the secrets and the pain, the anxieties, traumas, and the failures they have experienced. These are the memories from an honest reflection on life within the family structure. These recollections run the gamut, from loving, caring families to outright abusive ones with lots of pain and suffering. I hear what people really think about the quality of their lives and the people in it.

The gathering of all these life stories leads to an understanding of how people measure their lives by either reaching their expectations or not reaching them. The "it" factor is constantly being defined and redefined in these sessions. Think of it as theatre where every person plays a role. Everyone wears a mask and, at some point, the mask is removed and the real true person is revealed. The therapist's job is to help the patient remove his own mask.

What if you were a priest or a rabbi and you were to serve as a moral guidepost for your community? You make all the orations at births, weddings, and funerals. You give sermons to the assembled. You comfort the sick and those in pain. You walk with pride in your community and are given special status. But what if you have a problem and you are hurting people with that problem? What if you can't control yourself and are taking advantage of children by manipulating them with your trust? What if you are using them for your own sexual needs? How do you live without your mask?

So many people in high-ranking positions do things that make them despise themselves—so much so they can't face self-discovery. They struggle with therapy, for fear of a worse self-discovery or, in some cases, legal repercussions.

Many people in this category have lost "it". They start out wanting to do good and make a difference, and they wind up doing much worse—to themselves and others. You can think of many people in important community roles who have failed themselves and whom they are supposed to protect: from teachers to police officers, to attorneys and judges; from safety control examiners to those who in some way represent doing the right thing the right way. When they violate themselves, they harm the community they serve, and the people have no idea what or who is behind the mask.

Most of the "it" here comes down to "I want it", "I have it", "I lost it", "I need it", "I can't have it", "I made it", "I abused it",

"I took advantage of it", "I don't know what 'it' is, anymore", and so on.

My experience has taught me that if you think "it" is a formula you can check off as you go along, then it's most likely not going to do the job for you. For example, I treated so many guys who went to dental school because their parents convinced them it was a respectable, professional job where they could make a good buck. It doesn't hurt that they called themselves "Doctor" when it came to dating. They could buy a house, raise kids, take them on fancy vacations. (You could substitute general practitioners, lawyers, architects, CPAs or Wall Street brokers and a multitude of others for the dentist).

So, what's wrong, you ask? Ask *them*. I did. It comes down to it being a script: do this, then that, and then this will happen. Except, what if you get fifteen years into the formula and you hate being a dentist, looking into people's mouths all day long? You are on your feet all day or leaning over constantly and have developed back problems. Your wife hates the long hours and the emergencies that pull you away from family. And then, the money isn't as good as you thought it would be with the costly malpractice insurance and overhead. Finding reliable, qualified staff is also a challenge.

Dentists are more prone to drug abuse than most other professions. More and more cases of dental/physician substance abuse are reported every year—not to mention the suicide rate. It comes down to the formula they bought into before going to college. They didn't have a back-up plan when they realized that they did every single thing they were supposed to do—and it didn't work. They didn't find "'it". What they found was that they borrowed so much money to complete their educations and certifications that they were in a deep financial hole before they even acquired a home or an office. When the pressure set in with competition in the field, they felt overwhelmed and miserable. An unhappy wife added to the dilemma. To sum it up, the parental advice was wrong. These guys were miserable, frustrated, and confused.

Remember when women were encouraged NOT to get an education, but to get a husband? "Get married, buy a home, have children, and you will be fulfilled forever". Then the husband takes her for granted and she never gets beyond being someone's wife or mother. The kids grow up, leave home, and suddenly the husband has found someone younger.

The Wall Street guys have a term: "the Golden Handcuffs". They make the money, but what they have to do to make it starts to erode their self-esteem. To the outside world, they are models of success: the big house, tons of help, big car, the "club", and the fancy international vacations. Their social circles are big and it's "cocktail time" all the time.

So, what's wrong? They spend their lives with "the company" and the rules of corporate life. The constant travel and pressure to deliver wears them down. They can never just "be". At work, they are toeing the line all the time and when they do finally get home they want to relax, but here comes all the obligations of marriage, family, community, and child-rearing. When the wife wants him to take over the tasks that she has been doing in his absence, he understands, but starts to feel he is just not in control of his life. Duties are everywhere.

All the accoutrements are there, but he just wants to find some peace and quiet and not have to do anything. Impossible. So, he retreats into having a few more drinks, or for some "zip" he starts to meet women while traveling. Now, things are getting out of control and he wants to get off the merry-go-round.

Here is where the "golden handcuffs" come in: the money. He needs the income for the lifestyle, and unless he has stashed a whole bundle of it by good investing, he's trapped. He rationalizes that it will be only a few more years. So, he comes to his first session and says, "I am not who they think I am—my life is a front, it sucks, and I'm unhappy. I have everything I thought I ever wanted, and it means nothing. I am making all those around me miserable."

Actually, it's better for the broker/Wall Street guy because he has more money and connections than the dentist and has built a bevy of personal relationships that can help him transition. The dentist has been isolated in his office, filling teeth, and has neither the connections nor the transferable skill set to start over.

The most responsive, transition-needing person I ever treated was a corporate lawyer. He absolutely hated what he did because he had some ethics and saw what his work did to those who were effected by his law firms' actions. He felt that all he did was hurt people. He wanted to stop.

He came to me to find his true self, his "it". He gave all the reasons why the "golden handcuffs" applied to him. He knew nothing else but corporate board room tasks and responsibilities because he was tied into what the firm wanted him to do. He was good at it, and therefore the cycle repeated itself for each new acquisition. It was the same thing over and over.

We started to explore what he liked and, after a long search, we discovered that what made him smile was working with his hands. As a child, he used to love to play in his father's basement tool room. They had built little boats and cars and repaired household items.

I told him he should consider starting weekend projects working with his hands. He gave a lot of "Yes, buts" and said he didn't see how that would solve the bigger problem. I held my ground and said, "You have to start somewhere—consider this a start."

It took a while, but one day he came in excited and said he had gone antique-hunting and had found a desk that needed fixing up. He brought it home and started stripping it, then sanding it. He bought some furniture repair books. Then, he looked at how to refinish it and, lo and behold, it came out nicely. He was both proud and happy. I focused on the happy part as he showed me a picture.

He became a weekend scavenger warrior, picking up pieces at farm auctions or wherever. He saw that he could make some money buying, refinishing, and selling. He began to hate the corporate job more and more. He debated long and hard, finally crunching his numbers and finding if he quit his job and sold his house, he and his family could move to a farmhouse on someone else's property. He had discovered the place during his antique-searching and the rent was cheap. He would also have use of the old man's tool shed.

He eventually left the firm and moved into the farmhouse. He then leased a store front in town, where he and his apprentice sold his refinished furniture. He got better at his choices and upped his skill level at stripping and refinishing. He also got free help from the local high school, as they got credit for "working" with him. This connection brought in a whole crowd of customers. Within a year, he was a new man, living a very different life where he was popular, doing what he liked and finding satisfaction in doing it. He would write me from time to time, and I watched him grow into a well-respected community member with a thriving business and a solid apprentice program. He told me he was so much happier now and only needed what he needed. He had found "it"—and he never looked back. He sent me other people over the years with the message, "Do for them what you did for me".

Dusting Off the Diamond

I have heard so many stories from people who lamented losing someone whom they had let go in their past. What is it about our search for "it" that allows us to reject, maltreat, or take for granted perfectly good partners who have done nothing to deserve being deemed "not enough"? Here is another composition example of guys who roughly had commitment issues with women.

Let's call him Mark. He was thirty-three and had a good job on Wall Street. He was not a "big bucks" guy at that moment, but he had potential. He did a lot of dating, but never seemed satisfied. His longest relationship lasted just over one year. He came to therapy because his friends had told him he was a perfectionist and it was a problem he should address.

The difficulty in treating a perfectionist is that it boils down to a value system decision and not necessarily a mental health issue. It's really only a problem if the client finds their own perfectionism getting in the way of any goal they set for themselves. One cannot convince a perfectionist that they have a problem because they will tell you that they are only doing things correctly and they are doing it better than everyone else. Who can argue that not making errors at work is better than making them? Or looking bad is better than looking good? Or finding your match is worse than "settling" for someone who isn't? The arguments quickly fall into the value system category and therapy proves ineffective—until the client realizes they are not happy with how their life is turning out.

Mark had broken up with "Carol" about four months before he came into the office. She was about five years younger than he, and made a good salary working for a software company. She was intelligent and came from a well- respected family. They had been dating about nine months when he started to feel less for her. This was a long-standing pattern for Mark, in that when he dated only one woman, he soon became disinterested. His friends really liked Carol and felt she was "a real catch".

Mark complained that Carol talked a lot and kept asking him how he felt about her. When I asked him why he thought she was posing that question so frequently, he responded that she was "insecure". He also complained that she wanted to spend more time socializing as a couple, whereas he preferred to stay home after a busy week and just be with her. He liked having sex with Carol, but she "wanted to do other things as well".

As time went on, Mark became annoyed that Carol was repeating the same things over and over. What was really going on was that he was not taking in what she was saying, nor was he considering his role in the problems of their relationship.

After he broke up with Carol, Mark felt relief, initially. But after one month he started to miss her and thought about her every day. He received no support from his friends, who accused him of "dumping" her. This was when the discussions over his perfectionism began.

As we worked our way in the therapeutic process, Mark started to look at, with my guidance, why he thought the problem was Carol and not him. My view was that she asked those questions because she correctly felt that he was exhibiting less affection for her. Mark finally identified a pattern within himself that told him he could "do better" with another woman. Now, that was a tough call. Sometimes it's true that one could be better matched, and other times it's more of an indication of a disturbing, self-defeating problem of entitlement and perfectionism.

I asked Mark to look at why he thought he could see Carol's good qualities in retrospect, when he had dismissed them while he was dating her. Eventually, we got to the real issue of what was causing his discontentment. Mark was more of a narcissist than a perfectionist, which meant he processed all information only through his own view and that never included looking at himself from another person's vantage point. It was difficult for him to see himself in what therapists call "the third eye view". This view is the imaginary camera in the corner of the room that sees both people talking and can describe and record for playback what it has observed. The non-verbal behavior is what breaks up the logjam in the narcissist's me only view. They see themselves for the first time as overly controlling and critical. It can be the first breakthrough in seeing that the problem exists in unrealistic expectations.

I asked Mark if he could meet the standard he sets for others? Over time, he realized he was measuring everything by what his parents had set for him as a standard for any potential partner. Turns out his mother had "settled" for his father and consequently lamented her choice for years. She was going to make sure Mark didn't make the same mistake. I told him that she had succeeded in solving her problem through him, but now he was suffering because of it. Tricky value system issues kept coming up, combined with issues of perfectionism and narcissism. Somewhere in there was a bottom-line balance of setting realistic expectations. There go those boundaries again.

Mark started to become aware that he was not the partner he thought he was. It was difficult for him to fight against what he had been taught in order to value others more and view his own narcissism as the problem, but he did. We used the metaphor that, in order to see the diamond underneath, you first have to dust it off. Then, "it" will be revealed. Mark agreed he was throwing away diamonds. His friends in turn applauded his change in self-perception. We laughed when Mark finally admitted that he was the one who needed some "dusting off".

Conversations About "It"

Observed at a taco stand in Guadalajara, Mexico: A young man in his mid-twenties had just ordered three *bistec* tacos with cheese, chili peppers, onions, and hot green salsa sauce. These were very substantial tacos, not like the little ones generally sold. When he received his order on a large tray, he stayed in position and took his first bite. *"Caramba!"* he shouted. He then told everyone nearby that he had been in jail for three years, dreaming about this moment. He yelled, "This is it! The best feeling I could ever hope for!" Everyone clapped for him as he ate his tacos with pure joy.

In Munich, Germany, after drinking too many beers during Octoberfest, an inebriated tourist drove his Alfa Romeo sports car onto the trolley tracks. At the crossing, the tracks were even with the roadbed, but that soon changed as the roadbed faded away, leaving only the tracks.

The man had turned prematurely and was now sitting squarely on the tracks. Out of nowhere, four German men rushed to the confused tourist and ordered him out of the car. They pushed the car back to where the roadbed was now even with the tracks. One man then got in the car and drove away.

The tourist yelled, "Stop, thief!" He turned to the other men and pleaded with them to call the police. "He is the police," one of the men said of the thief. "This happens quite often, and he is just driving the car around the block to make sure it is ok. He doesn't get a chance to drive an Alfa very often and 'it' is fun."

At an unmarked intersection in the middle of nowhere in southern Utah stood a tiny general store. Two men stood outside near the gas pump, talking.

"Which way to Bryce Canyon?" asked one.

"Don't know it," the other replied, "but which way did you come from?"

The man pointed east.

"Well, so it ain't thataway," the man replied. "I came from the north, and it ain't thataway neither. So, you can pick from the other two directions—one of them will be right." The man walked to his car and drove off.

The mystified traveler asked me if I knew, and I replied that I didn't. I suggested he go inside and ask the store's proprietor. The old man behind the counter said he knew it. "Used to be a sign out front pointing the way, but it got old and fell down," he commented.

"Which way did it point?" the traveler asked.

"West or south. Can't really say which road is better, but you have to take both to get there."

The traveler gave the old man a confused look. "What?"

"The canyon is southwest of here," the old man replied. "Whichever road you take first, take the other next. 'It' will be in front of you." …

Late night in a bar in New Orleans, a soused man leans forward and asked the bartender, "How much does 'it' cost around here?"

"Well, that depends on what 'it' is," the bartender replied.

"The usual," the drunk said. "You know."

"You talking drugs or sex?" the bartender asked.

"Um … sex."

"What kind?"

"What kind of sex?"

"Yes," the bartender said. "You want men or women?"

"Women."

"What do you want them to do?"

"Geez, I don't know," the drunk replied. "Is there a menu or something I can pick from?"

"Well, in order to fulfill your request, I need to know what you want."

"Well," the drunk replied cautiously, "I just want to—you know—put it in."

"In what?" asked the bartender.

"Is there something funny going on here?" the drunk said impatiently. "I just want to have regular sex with a woman."

"Young or old?"

"Damn, I don't know! Young, I guess."

"Legal age or younger?"

"Legal. Got to be legal."

"Well, what you are wanting is not legal to begin with, so the age doesn't really matter, does it?"

"Ok, I want an above legal age, say, eighteen-year-old woman, to have straight intercourse. Is that enough information?"

"Yes, it is."

The bartender went to a phone and made a call. But he never returned to the drunk man, who was waiting patiently.

"Excuse me," he said finally, "how much will 'it' cost?"

"It's free," the bartender replied.

The drunk smiled. "Well," I like that! Where is she?"

"She's out back, by the tractor trailer."

"Never heard of it being free," the drunk says as he leaves, "but I'll give it a try."

Ten minutes later, he returns.

"I didn't find anybody out there."

"Is that so?" said the bartender. "Well, it didn't cost you anything, did it?"

"No, it didn't" the drunk man replied.

"And you just got screwed, didn't you?"

Bartender turns to the other patrons and puts his arms out, like a magician does after completing his trick. Right on cue they all applauded. "It's" not easy in the Big Easy if you are drunk.

I was introduced to Mai Ka Bei, a forty-one-year-old female elephant and grand dame of the entire herd in Chang Mai, Thailand. She was the largest of all the elephants in the sanctuary. I was instructed to just stand in front of her and let her check me out. She looked right at me, and then used her trunk to scan me up and down.

The trainer said, "If you pass the smell test, she will drop her trunk and then raise it towards you, so you can feed her some bananas." I passed, and she accepted my bananas. We then walked to a stream and she went in and knelt. With large palm leaves, I brushed the dirt off her and then splashed her with pails of water. With large sponges, I cleaned her mammoth body. She sprayed me with water, showing her appreciation and sense of humor. After the bath, we walked to the official staging area. Here was the final test.

I was allowed once again to feed Mai Ka Bei. She wrapped her trunk around me and gave me a little twist. She was having fun. I had not one iota of fear—the huge elephant was kind and funny. She again gave me the smell test. The trainer said, "If she continues to like you, she will kneel and turn her right foot skyward. If she does that, step up on her foot and she will lift you high enough so you can climb up using the rope on her back."

I did as the trainer said and it was magical: the two-ton pachyderm lifted me onto her back. I was instructed to place my knees behind her ears and sit as far forward as I could. I was now ten feet off the ground.

We formed a caravan and went on a four-hour walk in the woods. It's hard to describe the feeling of riding an elephant bareback—it surpassed everything I had ever done. I talked to Mai Ke Bei all afternoon. She would pause to pull up some reeds and stop by the stream when she was thirsty. She bounced along at a steady pace, and when she felt like upping it, she did. She spoke Thai and I was given the words for "Go" and "Stop". When the day was over, she again knelt and put the foot in place to help me down. I then walked with her, holding her trunk with my arms. She would wiggle it playfully. At one point, I walked a little ahead of her and I swear she goosed me with her trunk. We had a spiritual goodbye talk as I told her what a magnificent animal she was. I could see she was looking directly at me. I got chills. She went back to her pail of water and gave me one more spritz for the road. The trainer told me that she felt me, and that I had earned her trust. Her behavior signaled that I had "it". The feeling was mutual …

I was at a ranch outside Cheyenne, Wyoming, talking to a cowboy as we watched a bronco being ridden for the first time—or at least the other cowboy was trying to ride it. My companion says, "What the heck is it about livin' in big cities with you folk? I mean, you have everything you need right here in the wide-open spaces. Ya got good air, plenty of different weather and enough room to breathe."

"You make a good point," I replied. "You don't mind freezing in the winter or dealing with snow drifts bigger than barns. You don't mind driving twenty-five miles to go to the store. You don't miss the theatre or being able to get from uptown to downtown by subway in ten minutes. You don't ever have to choose between forty different countries' restaurants for dinner. You don't miss seeing every different culture, all living within eight miles of one another—"

"And," he added, "I don't have to deal with smog, traffic congestion that is just plain inhuman, lines to go everywhere and paying forty dollars for one person for dinner."

"True enough, but what if you like sushi?"

The cowboy wrinkled his nose. "Now, why the hell would anyone in their right mind like that?"

"What about ten different types of pizza, or a gelato station that sells twenty flavors?"

"Something wrong with vanilla or chocolate?"

"No, but it comes with the turf in big cities—you get choices, lots of them."

"Not me," the cowboy said, "I like this simple life where things are regular and have a rhythm to them, like sunsets and sunrises."

I looked at him and smiled. "In case you don't know, we have them in the East as well."

"Yeah, but you don't see 'em with all those big buildings— makes no sense at all to live thataway."

"I can see your point—that's why I leave it and come here."

"My point exactly," he says. "You have to leave to find it, and I have it all the time. I don't need to leave."

"So, you never played stick ball in the summer on the sweltering street, with a bunch of your friends, and got to hit a two-sewer home run and talk about it all week?"

"Well, you never worked all day birthing a calf then rode into town with your buddies on horses and got to shoot pool, drink some beers, and eat a steak with men who really appreciate their time off."

"Alls I can say is, if that is what "it" is for you, then who am I to say anything?"

"Different is as different gets," was his answer.

"It" worked for both of us.

"It" Can be Found in Failure

Initially, I didn't understand it: how could failure be good for anyone? Yet, all the books I read by successful men kept saying that failure was part of the process to succeeding. Even the professional boxers had a slant on it: "It doesn't matter if they knock you down," they said. "What matters is your attitude when you get back up."

So many young people suffer from "fear of failure" that they never give themselves a chance to overcome the fear. How many guys refuse to walk across a room and ask a girl to dance or talk for fear of rejection or humiliation? But, like most adages that are true, if you don't buy the lottery ticket, you guarantee you will never hit the jackpot. I knew so many guys who froze at social occasions. They would eye a girl from afar but never initiate a conversation.

Or, they would stand around in a bar and gape at someone but do nothing—except lament about the guy who left with the person in question.

Fear of rejection has deep roots for a lot of people. It prevents growth and fosters more anxiety than the reality of trying would ever produce. If they at least gave it a shot and it didn't work out, they could say they tried. It's a step in the right direction.

Let's examine some failures. I knew an actor who used to get only bit parts in movies. He, like most actors, waited tables or bar-tended to make "survival" money. He would go to "cattle calls" to audition, but he never got that "money call" for the big role. He grew despondent over the years and began to drink more and sleep less. The result was predictable: He felt like he was a failure and started to act that way. He was becoming a burden to his friends because he was always feeling sorry for himself. When they staged an intervention, telling him to give up acting and try something else, he eventually picked up a camera.

He began taking photographs—good ones—with an artistic flair. He worked his way up to a one-man show in Soho, receiving rave reviews. Then came the photo book. He began doing magazine and newspaper interviews, wherein he showed his dynamic sense of humor. Soon, he caught the eye of a member of a British comedy group, who had remembered him from his acting days. Liking his dry wit, the person asked him to try out for the comedy team.

He was an instant success as he relied on the failed actor routine now as a comedy bit. After a series of runs in the US and England, he returned to New York and started his own theatre group and performed off-Broadway while periodically performing with the

British group. I saw one of his TV interviews where he praised failure as the necessary ingredient for his success, as he wanted everyone to know not to give up if you fail.

His story parallels many entrepreneurs who have failed at business, only to learn from their mistakes and try again. Sometimes it took three or four attempts before they got it right. Look at some figures in professional sports: how many stories have you heard about baseball players languishing in the minor leagues, until some turn of events occurs, and they get their shot at the majors? Similarly, how many politicians have you known who lost their first election but then came back to win the next one?

On a more personal note, when I was working for Falcon Eddie, whom I mentioned earlier in the book, I had failed out of college and was forced to work for this shyster. I felt like a total failure. I was a smart kid who had been working in factories, cleaning bathrooms, and now I was selling bibles door-to-door for a con-man. Meanwhile, my friends were doing well in college and spending their summers traveling.

Bottom line to my story is that, once I finished the reparative college/work period, I did get my degree. The factor that saved me was that I got drafted into the Army and was sent to Germany instead of Vietnam. I was trained in psychiatric social work instead of being shot at. That turnaround and military training eventually got me a free scholarship at Columbia University for my Masters, with nothing but success afterward. Failure? I knew it well, along with poverty. It made me never want to see it again.

In terms of "failure", one of the most positive people I ever met was a forty-year-old woman whom I met in the Village at our yoga center. She was getting married and wanted a "good sounding board" before she said, "I do". When I heard her history, I understood why she wanted a sounding board.

She had been married three times before. The first marriage was her method of escape from an abusive childhood home. She referred to herself as "naïve" and "desperate" in those years—her only desire was to get out of the house.

Like the girl who hops on the back of a motorcycle to get away—until she stops in the next town and realizes just whose motorcycle she jumped on—the marriage lasted one year. She realized she was too young to be married and got a job, went to night school, and eventually became a nurse.

At age twenty-seven she married a "good man" who, unbeknownst to her, had a secret. Eighteen months later she discovered he was a bisexual who thought he could "go straight" by getting married. She wanted to save her marriage and insisted he get counseling. The therapist told him that bisexuality is not an issue for treatment. It was what it was.

She could neither share him nor change him, so she divorced him. Consequently, she became extremely cautious whenever she dated, demanding to know if her dates had any secrets. At thirty-two, she married a wealthy stockbroker. They lived comfortably in a big house and she had a daughter. In the fourth year of marriage, her husband was convicted of securities fraud and, before being sent to prison, he took his own life. She was shattered, needing medication and therapy.

This woman told me that she did nothing wrong in marriages two and three and that the divorce and widowhood had helped her to stand up for herself. She did not blame herself for those relationships. Now, she had met a hard-working widower with a young son. She finally stopped grilling him when he told her she needed to find her "present" as he was not her past but rather her future.

She said life had taught her about "it", and "it" had not always been easy. She said she was a good woman whose track record didn't look good on paper. She felt she had learned what she needed to learn and wanted to move forward with this good man, get married, and have another child.

It is always refreshing to meet people who have hit many bumps in the road but continue to travel it with optimism and hope. I told her that she sounded sure of herself and I wished her well in her new marriage.

"It" is Not in the Bottle

"Oh, yes it is!" cry my Irish drinking friends. What would life be like without the camaraderie of friends telling stories over a few pints? It never stopped Sean O'Casey from writing. My friends cite example after example of successful men and women who have drunk and often drunk heavily.

True enough. Well, my Irish friends tend to justify their own behavior with non-clinical, nice-sounding story snippets. But over the long haul, the bottle will bring them down, because that's just the way it is. The "it" you get is short-term. You can watch it play out in one night or in one life—it's all the same.

I saw alcohol from three very clear perspectives. The first was as a bartender in the West Village, at that famous Irish story-telling saloon, the fabulous White Horse Tavern. The other was from the Emergency Room at Beth Israel Hospital in NYC, and the Emergency Room at Elizabeth General Medical Center. Then, I saw it from my office as a family therapist.

Here's the basic, one-night bartender view: people come in with smiles in a good mood. They are looking forward to a fun night of talking, eating, and drinking. After one round, there is not much of a noticeable difference. The second round brings changes as people become louder, depending on their tolerance. This also depends on what is being served. Hard liquor like whisky or vodka speeds up the process. In this case, I'm referring to beer and wine. After the third round, people are feeling less self-conscious: some are more gregarious and telling personal stories. Inhibitions have diminished.

Some are starting to show the first signs of being drunk: wobbling when they walk or telling tangential stories. By the fourth round, there are mood changes: some irritability and argumentativeness. Some people begin to withdraw as the effects take over. There is heightened sensitivity and misperceptions occur. The clients with insecurities are the most obvious. They feel competitive or overlooked, and arguments begin. By the fifth round, only real drinkers are still standing. When they reach this point, they are all legally drunk and this is when it gets dangerous. If they switch to hard liquor now, there will be negative results. Logical thinking is replaced by emotional reactions and reality testing is impaired. Bar fights occur at this stage. Any further drinking and it's all downhill. Bodies start to lose balance and minds lose objectivity. Some become ill and others will fade into the first stages of sleep. Those who go beyond this are chronic drinkers and can still manage to fake it, but if they were given a driving test, they would knock down all the cones.

From here on out it can get ugly. People start to rant nonsense and have no ability to listen. They just ramble on, talking to no one in particular. If they slow down now, they can make it almost to closing time, when their heads will be on the bar, some of them crying.

They start off happy, feel better at first, and then proceed down a slippery slope. At the end of the evening, the person is alone and listens to no one. Only an authority figure can get results, and that comes with a lot of jibberish and patently emotional confabulation. It's not pretty. Some people laugh at this person. Movies play it up. They shouldn't. It's serious.

The life story bottle saga is the same. One starts out ok—girl-friend, boyfriend, house, children, community—and then, be-cause of the drinking, the problems increase, and productivity goes down. The more drinking, the more losses. Friendships and inti-mate relationships suffer, as does job performance. Now the lying, denial, and cover-ups ensue, and the first real consequences appear.

The problem is noticeable. Choice and change need to be implemented because, if not now, the decline begins in earnest. It can be with health or psychological issues and usually both. Losses mount up: relationships, jobs. Friends and family begin to distance themselves. To get by the denial and face the truth is now critical. Addiction has set in. It can be compounded by psychiatric disor-ders, such as manic depression. This category of patient tends to self-medicate as alcohol temporarily soothes the fire inside.

It can be years before a person "hits the wall". Some people find themselves in legal trouble with DUIs and possibly fatal accidents.

The bottom is lonely. At this stage it's either detox and rehab, meetings and commitment, or the downward slide of self-destruction.

I have seen so many families devastated by alcohol, and if there is an alcoholic in the family, every member is affected. It is critical for non-alcoholic family members to get their own support. "I can't make you drink, and I can't make you stop" is Day One. The consequences need to be redirected back to the drinker and not to those who love him/her. It's tough work, because there can be major changes in the family dynamic due to loss of income or other consequences.

People must learn that addiction is its own entity, and it overtakes a person until they choose to rid themselves of active participation in its growth. This is why meetings are so important—the person sees that they are not alone as they listen to others' experiences. They learn to love but set boundaries and keep them, no matter what. Alcoholism will always be there, and a lifetime commitment to change is the only way to challenge it. The younger the person, the better the chances.

Just like that happy bar crowd of young drinkers, a short phase is fine. But if it becomes a lifestyle, your goose is cooked. "It" will take your life away from you.

You not only can't find "it" in a bottle, you also can't find it in cheesecakes, hamburgers, ice cream, or anything else you eat too much of. You also can't find it with sex, no matter how much of it you let yourself have. That also goes for a zillion items purchased from Home Shopping Network or QVC. No matter how much you buy or how many packages come to the house, you will not find it there. And money: no matter how much you have it only buys external things—and there is always more to buy. How many rich or famous people have fallen to addiction when they had everything one could desire? "If I only had some (fill in the blank), then everything would be fine". No. You get to a point where you are fine with what you have, or the cycle continues. The only thing you can't get more of is time, so don't go chasing "it".

Despite What You Think, Money isn't "It"

How much time do people spend chasing money in order to find "it"? Just stand next to the lottery line and listen to what people are saying. They play almost daily: "lucky" numbers or numbers with special meaning are scrolled into combinations by people of little means looking for their big payday. They talk about what they would do with their winnings, most saying they would only spend it on one or two limited items—a different view from that of people who already have money. People with money know that you need a managed plan in your life or things can get very complicated.

This is not to say that money can't take away a lot of worry about day-to-day life; but having money isn't always a blessing. People not used to having money who hit the lottery often experience disaster. It depends on the windfall, but I'm referring generally to poor people who hit in the two million range. Everyone around them overestimates the distance that money will go. If you thought your friends were needy, watch what happens now that everyone knows you are "rich". I have read too many stories about professional boxers who made millions of dollars in the ring but wound up broke. It's all about understanding money and how to manage it. You can't acquire it, spend like crazy, and still think you have it. Look at the musicians who made millions but wound up destitute. It's sad when a person's ship comes in and then you see it slip over the horizon.

The value of money is directly related to how you use it. Some will put a secure portion away for the future, hopefully wisely invested. They will then spend it on stable, asset-gaining investments like real estate. Add some creature comforts and one can start to feel good. Young people with windfalls are dangerous. Many of them buy overpriced sports cars and, due to their immaturity, wind up wrapped around a telephone pole, Hollywood style.

Money, and the pursuit of it, can become all-consuming. It really depends on the quality of your life prior to your acquisition. I have worked with poor people—not all are unhappy and desperate as some depict them. They can be perfectly content to live within their means, especially if they are surrounded by good family relationships and love. I think the toughest position to be in with regard to money is to have some and yet constantly want more. It's a seductive process. How many people do you know who moved into a bigger house and yet they were not happy? Bills went up, and so did expectations. The result was less contentment.

People without money think all their problems will be solved *with* money. They are correct in assuming that some of their problems will be solved, but they will be replaced by new ones. For example, the fortunate ones will begin to receive unsolicited requests for help. They must decide whom to help and how much to give them. They listen to heart-breaking stories and are torn over what to do. They can begin to lose sleep. Sometimes, if they quit their jobs, their lives become all about managing their money. Sudden retirement can produce anxiety over time allocation, if they have nowhere to go during the day.

Friends and relatives may start to view you differently. I knew one man whose friends assumed the bill would automatically find its way to him. He resented it after a time and experienced conflict because he did not want to say anything for fear of being thought of as miserly. His children's friends started to call them "rich kids". Sometimes, people who get a windfall get depressed because what they thought would happen to their lives simply did not happen. They still had the same friends, but that can be either good or bad. Newfound friends can be friends of the money and not the person who has it. Ask people who own a pool—they have lots of friends on hot summer days.

Many people experience scrutiny from friends or family because of how they spend or don't spend the money. Perhaps, prior to their new wealth, the person or persons were "off the radar", only to now find themselves "front and center". Maybe they preferred the quiet.

What "it" is without money is just different than what it is with it. Sometimes better, sometimes worse. "It" depends on so many unforeseen factors. People write a lot of books to help others save, spend, and manage money. Life doesn't simply get better just because a person suddenly acquires riches.

Setting Boundaries

Some of the toughest lessons in learning to be a therapist come from the inability to make or keep a boundary. Simply defined, it's where I end and you begin. Symbiosis is the opposite of good boundaries. It is two people living as one. More moderate examples are people with personality disorders, and what the books call *undifferentiated egos*. Prime examples are borderline personality disorders, where people exhibit major trust issues around separation and individuation. They suffer from abandonment and basic trust deficiencies. After a while, a good therapist can "feel" their presence. A quick way to know is when you find yourself doing things for this patient that seem rushed or unusual. For them, it's all about "proving" to them that you can be trusted. Borderlines are skilled in manipulation. Having minimal internal trust, they manage by manipulating the external world to limit their own exposure to normal trust issues. Just like an anxiety patient who has everyone running around trying to help them not feel nervous, when it's really their job to calm themselves down.

Another clue is how quickly a borderline can turn on a dime to becoming angry and critically demeaning. They are exhibiting what happened to them. Narcissistic and overly critical parents can raise borderline children very easily. Children deprived of normal validation and respect develop a shell around an "undeserving" sense of self. It is brutal for them to expose themselves to issues of trust, for they fear historical repetition of their original hurt, criticism, and ultimately emotional abandonment. They can be very bright, charming, and very clear in their views of what is wrong with others.

One must set up a consistent boundary which says, "It's what you want me to do but not what I want to do". Your need, my need. Your projection of who I am and my knowledge of who I am. Setting a clear boundary between doctor and patient is mandatory. This is not two friends talking.

Sessions have time limits and management of the time and content is also a patient's responsibility. Needing more time on a specific day has nothing to do with caring, despite what they say to you. Learning to say "don't bring up big issues at the end of the session" is their responsibility. Saying, "We won't have enough time for this in today's session" is the best response. You will be tested time and time again.

My first borderline patient yelled at me for months on end, so much so that the staff thought I was being too lenient. She was very loud and very critical. I told them she needed time to see that I could take it and wouldn't retaliate. "She's not used to non-retaliation and it drives her nuts that I don't yell back. She'll learn at some point." It took a long time, but finally she said, "I've been thinking that I expect you to be like my mother, and I see now you are not, and I am sorry for my treatment of you. I would have thrown me outta here if I were you." I simply said, "It wouldn't have helped you." She replied, "I guess I was pushing to see how far I could go—thanks for not doing that." "You are welcome" was my necessary response, as this interaction was important to her relearning, and a positive response showed appreciation and reinforcement. Boundary number one established.

I learned many skills while working in the Psychiatric Emergency Room of Hospitals. The basic task is to triage. It's about intervention and the choices that comprise it. In the military, in the field, you assess in order to sort out variables. Group One is those who will live and get better without your immediate help. Group Two is those who are beyond your ability to help, as they will die no matter what you do. That leaves the group that says they will survive only *with* your help.

Emergency Room triage is to send home those who do not need your help. Group Two is to intervene with medicine and/or emergency counseling and outpatient follow-up. Group Three needs immediate admission to Psych.

I will never ever forget (I'll call him) Jacques. He was a big Haitian man with large facial features and the biggest lips I had ever seen. When he spoke fast, the lips could never keep up and he was difficult to understand with his thick, Haitian accent. When he came into the ER on a Saturday night with his entire extended family, he was agitated, nervous, pacing, and periodically crying. The family really loved this man. They said he was a terrific, kind and caring family man. Now, he was perseverating about "Papa

Doc" Duvalier, the notorious dictator of Haiti. Jacques had recently arrived from Haiti, fleeing the feared dictator who was known to spy on his own people. Vans would show up in the middle of the night and take people to prison.

Jacques was not a political refugee, as he had been a carpenter in Haiti with no affiliations to underground groups. When he flew out of Port-au-Prince, he saw Papa Doc talking on the television about the "rats who are escaping Haiti". He was like so many others with that similar condition, living in fear of a dictator.

Now, ten days later, Jacques was clearly delusional and clinically paranoid—he saw "Papa Doc" everywhere. Any wire or overhead electronic junction box became Papa Doc and his secret society. It was like the East German Stasi informing on their own citizens. There is always a particle of truth at the beginning of any paranoid chain. He did live in a country where people spied on one another. But it was a stretch to think the local telephone pole junction box had anything to do with what was going on in Haiti.

After talking for twenty minutes, I told Jacques I understood, and that he was safe. I told him he was beginning to lose touch with reality and scare his family. He gave me a giant hug and asked if I could help him. I described the process: he would be admitted and given medication, and then would be sent to our Day Hospital where I was also in charge of therapy. "I trust you, Mr. Ken." "I will protect you, Jacques," I replied. We hugged again as I guided this wonderfully fragile man to Admissions.

I visited him daily—the meds were working as reality began to seep back in between his fears. In seven days, he was no longer delusional, but his grip was not yet strong as his eyes still looked vulnerable. Jacques was sent on late Monday morning to the Day Hospital.

The Monday orientation for new patients had been done earlier. Patients were already in their group activities. When they walked Jacques over to the Day Hospital, the patient care coordinator was not at his desk. He would have explained the routine, privacy, and confidentiality issues and answered all questions. He would have obtained Jacques' written permission: a well-thought-out entry plan. But not if the coordinator was getting a cup of coffee. Jacques told the nurse escorting him that he was there to see Mr. Ken. Instead of telling him to sit and wait for the coordinator, she brought him to my group therapy session that was now in progress. I saw Jacques at the door, welcomed him, and introduced him to the group. I had no thought that he had not been processed correctly. As Jacques settled into the group, he told his "Papa Doc" story. Everyone felt for him.

Then, in a split second, his face changed, and he stood up and pointed at the mounted camera I used to tape the sessions. "What is that? Does that feed directly to Papa Doc? I am a dead man! I am a dead man!" He fled the room and I excused myself and went after him. Our connection from the ER was still good. I told him that it was my camera and that it was used for therapy purposes only. We sorted out what had happened earlier, and I said, "Remember me telling you that you were safe here? Let me show you I am telling you the truth."

He was white with panic, fearing Papa Doc had found him. I felt I owed it to him to show him the technicals. So, after the group had left the room, I took Jacques to the camera and showed him the wire which led up through the foam padded tiles of the ceiling into the video recording room next door. We then went into the video room and he saw the wire coming down directly to the taping machine. I popped out the cassette and we watched it. I told him the tape was my property and belonged to the Day Hospital. No one was allowed to see it as it was covered by doctor/patient confidentiality laws. He calmed down and cried as he hugged me once more.

We changed our policy about admitting clients to any group without their signed sheet in their hand. Jacques and I eventually were able to laugh together about the unfortunate chain of events that had set him off. Jacques made a full recovery and even finished out-patient weekly sessions with me. When it was all said and done, he and I shared a laugh about the almost tragic but yet comedic set of circumstances that we shared. He got a big kick our me telling him we called the new required signature form "Jacques". My lesson? Trust is the most essential ingredient in any relationship—especially in therapy.

The Truth Was Last

A man called my office requesting an early morning appointment because he had a Wall Street job and needed to catch the 8:15 train. I thought that a bit unusual, as Wall Streeters work early and usually request the last hour for their appointments. It's easier for them to be seen working early than walking in late, easier to slip out at 6:30. I gave him an early appointment.

Robert showed up on time—mid-thirties, married, with a two-year-old daughter. He was dressed well and was very pleasant. After some initial, usual conversation about confidentiality and payment, I asked what brought him in. He told me he was having a problem with his job, that he didn't like what he was doing and thought his immediate supervisor was making life tough for him. We explored that history and then I focused on his personal family history, gathering information about relationships, past and present. He seemed transparent in his responses to my questions and I sensed nothing out of the ordinary. When I asked about his marriage, he said it was good, but that his wife was having some adjustment issues as she was also a Wall Streeter who had left her job to become a full-time mother.

His wife, Cindy, was feeling isolated and had started to complain that he didn't understand what this change has meant for her, because he hadn't changed anything in his life. He said he wished she would go back to work as they could afford a nanny.

The session followed a usual pattern of history-gathering and some discussion about what he was looking to accomplish in therapy. He said he had to solve his work dilemma, because he needed the job, but it was becoming more of a problem.

Robert had a few more sessions. Then, I received a call from Cindy, who asked for a session. I asked if she had told her husband that she was calling me. She said no. I told her that, for me to hear anything about her relationship with her husband, she would need to talk with him first. She said she would.

During my next session with him he said he had talked with Cindy about her wanting a session. He wondered why she had picked me. I asked if it were a marital issue and suggested they come in together. He said he would talk again with her.

The next week, Cindy called me again stating she wanted to come in by herself first, saying she and Robert had agreed that if marital issues were to be discussed, they would come together. I gave her an appointment.

Like her husband, Cindy was very friendly, open, and eager to answer all historical and personal questions. She was focused on her dramatic change from being a successful banker to being a stay-at-home mom with a toddler in the midst of the "terrible twos".

Robert was increasingly concerned about finances as he was not sure he could continue at his job and what that would mean for the family's ability to maintain their comfortable lifestyle. We talked about his possible search for another job, as he had ten years' banking experience.

Then, a very odd happenstance occurred. I had a luncheon date with a friend in a town about twenty minutes away. In the same café, sitting in a corner, totally absorbed with his computer, was Robert. This was around one in the afternoon, the time when, by his reports, he would be hard at work on Wall Street. I did not approach him, and I was certain he did not see me. I had lunch with my friend and left, thinking to myself, *What is he doing here?*

When I saw him the next week, I said nothing about the café incident. I instead inquired if his job required any travel, either local or international business. He said no, that he was chained to his desk all day.

Why would he not tell the truth? I had many choices as what to do with the information I had gathered by happenstance. I decided to be forthcoming.

Robert lost all color when I told him I had seen him that day in the café. He said he had taken a sick day and had gone there because he did not want his wife to know he wasn't at work. All my alarm bells went off. *Now he is lying to her and lying to me.* I said we needed a couple's session to ferret out the truth. He said no.

My next session with Cindy was one where all ethical issues presented themselves. I could not tell her I had seen Robert. I also could not discuss marital issues without both being present. I told her that I wanted a marital session with the two of them and asked her to discuss it with Robert. She agreed.

My next session with Robert would determine what the problem really was. I again requested a marital session, telling him that therapy was impossible without truth, and that if he were lying to her, I needed him to tell me why. "I have been telling a million lies," he admitted finally. "I can't take it anymore. I have to talk about it."

Robert told me that he'd lost his job four months before and hadn't been able to tell Cindy or anyone else. He would get up, get dressed, and leave the house each weekday as if he were still working. To keep her off track, he kept buying upgraded appliances for the home, but admitted that the credit card bills were getting out of control. He was increasingly having difficulty sleeping.

I asked him why he could not tell Cindy. He replied that his wife had lived through very bad times when her father had lost his job. When I asked him what his plan was, he said "To get a goddamned job! I've been networking for months and have had three interviews, but it's rough sledding out there right now—all the firms are downsizing and consolidating."

"Have you considered the damage you are doing to your relationship by not being truthful?" I asked him. He said he simply couldn't tell her. I told him I would strive to convince him it was the right thing to do. "The damage you are doing might be too much for Cindy," I said. "It's about basic trust."

I didn't have to strive for long: two weeks later, Cindy opened their bank statement and saw there had been no deposits. Furious, she confronted him. Two days later, she asked Robert to move out. Cindy felt violated by his months-long charade and his deception. His defense of "trying to protect her" only fueled her anger, as she felt he had been treating her like a child instead of an adult partner.

"It" was a secret which didn't have to be, and it eventually cost Robert his marriage as Cindy could never completely trust him again. The finances came to a crisis before he found a job for about half of what he had been making. Cindy returned to her old firm and downsized to an apartment. They divorced two years later.

Roughly Twelve
to Fourteen

When I was in practice as a family therapist, I gradually evolved to my specialty: treating families who had children in the roughly twelve-to-fourteen age range. Why, you ask? Because I found that was probably the most difficult stage in life for the child/adolescent and certainly for the family. It's the middle school years and everyone knows how upside down those years can be for the kids as well as parents. There are many reasons why this is a tough adjustment period for all involved. My belief was that if I could help families navigate these tough times of change, it could prevent far worse problems down the road.

Certainly, there are exceptions to what I am going to talk about—even the age range can change. I found that inner city kids, for whatever reason, seemed to start adolescence earlier than suburban or rural kids. Maybe it's their exposure to a larger population of older adolescents or the milk has more hormones, whatever, but city kids start to question the way things are a bit earlier.

In order to help kids (who were referred by the guidance office, a pediatrician, or juvenile services) survive the "cliquey", middle school years I saw the kids individually and in groups. They also attended family sessions to help set up a repair channel for broken communication. I also saw the parents without their pubescent offspring.

There are a lot of moving pieces in this equation. Some families are healthier than others, and some parents had better adolescent years than others. I found that trying to help moms and dads parent more effectively during these years was difficult due to many reasons, one being the hormone level in the house. Having more than one teenager really amps up the problem. Another big factor is the type of adolescence the parent had. If they had bad or absent parenting during their own adolescence, they were flying by the seats of their pants with no real road map. That was where I came in. I helped parents listen to their children more and talk less. Understanding beats lecturing every time.

Let's talk about what is going on with kids as they enter the early stages of the adult world and why these years are referred to as "upside down". First, it's the hormones. I will divide the conversation into boys and girls as they are very different in terms of what is going on with them.

With girls, it's hormones first. Whether the child is ready for adolescence is hurdle number one. That first menstrual cycle can be brutal, scary, and unwanted if the girl is not ready to begin womanhood. It can be a benchmark for entrance into the world of women, with lots of support as she joins the sorority. Girls who have the most problems with their changing bodies are ones who are fearful of growing up, with all the dangers that symbolic sexuality brings to the table. Men can be viewed as dangerous, as the world certainly proves that to be true. Boys can be viewed as threats to their safety and other girls can either be the support or the cause of undue pain, embarrassment, and ridicule.

Everyone has witnessed the cattiness and cruelty of adolescent girls as they choose friends and form groups or cliques. The competition and comparisons can be excruciating. The safest position to be in is in the middle of the continuum of changing bodies. If you are ahead of the pack, you can be singled out for attention or jeers. The same goes for the last to develop, the "late-bloomer". The issue here is integrating the new body and the first yens of sexuality into an ego that is not accustomed to the change. You are going to have a sexual body whether you want it or not. Some fight it like hell and cover up completely. The other end of the spectrum can be observed in the daily fights between mothers and daughters, with the mothers desperately trying to cover up the newly formed bodies that the teenagers want to show.

Usually based on popularity, groups now re-form and old friends can be discarded. This is rough for girls who have done nothing "wrong" but are seen as no longer "cool". Early sexual acting-out can bring huge popularity for all the wrong reasons. Many young girls have had to change schools for this behavior as their reputation is written on the internet.

Focusing on their home life was essential for girls going through this turbulence of change and adaptation. If you cannot talk at home and get support and guidance, then the isolation and criticism from peers can be unbearable. It's tough enough to talk to parents about unwanted or embarrassing feelings. Depending on the health of the parent, it can be a quagmire of bad advice, broken communication, and a hell of a lot of dishonesty. Remember, for teenagers these are the big years of lying. They embellish, make up, exaggerate, and confabulate their events into a whirlwind of truth, fantasy, wishes, and reality. The hormones make big issues small and, more commonly, small issues big.

With so many intertwining factors, it is the therapist's job to boil them down to a few treatable paradigms. It is difficult to gain mastery over unfamiliar emotions but being able to understand them and encourage teens to talk about them is essential. Acting out—the most common adolescent behavior that gets them into trouble—is putting into behavior what you can't put into words. My job was to help them find the words.

For the parents, it is a whole new world of change as their once docile and agreeable child now has temper tantrums and uses words never spoken in the house before. Depending on the external influences on the girls, parents can make so many mistakes like attacking their "new" friends or blaming them for what is going on with their daughter. It is much better to focus on the values being sought after by the teenager to help them see whether the current behavior is on track or not. Teenagers are vulnerable and they seek acceptance. If they don't get it at home, then the chance of it coming from external sources greatly increases. Not to paint a completely dark picture—everyone has gone through it, one way or the other. The old adage that you never get through adolescence without some scarring is quite true, but you do come out on the other side, hopefully.

The ones who don't are easily recognizable as they are the ones who never changed.

The most common household problem is parents who do not agree on what to say or do. This sets up the teenager's ability to split the middle and divide parental authority and is usually done along gender lines. Fathers are banned from conversations about bodies or emotions. Fathers can also undermine the mother's authority by labeling her as "emotional" or "having her own problems".

What is needed are four parental ears and one mouth. The parents need to huddle before they speak. It is ok to disagree, but the issue is what the teenager needs and not whether the parent thinks they are right. Advising your child to deal with it like you did is generally bad advice. The times have changed so much that parents have trouble keeping up with the "new normal" and the vernacular of the internet and its effect on the child's ability to personally interact and not text. If a parent does not understand the power of a group chat, this leads the teenager to say, "You don't understand anything" or "It's a waste of time talking to you so please leave my room". The teenage experience has changed so rapidly that books from two to three years ago are now dated. I usually, with a lot of resistance, get the child to run the playbook by the parents to help them understand more of what they are going through. Leaving a young teenager on the internet unsupervised is a negligent form of parenting. I tell parents that if they want to understand they have to monitor their teen's activity. The world is way more dangerous these days and supervision is mandatory. The kids with real problems are building arsenals from the internet and researching destructive and controlling websites.

The less frightening and more common teenage problems can

be viewed as transient and not permanent. Last year's desire to join a coven because she thought she was a witch has been replaced by wanting to join the girls' hockey team. If the parents can upgrade their tolerance level of new music and clothing styles, then there will be less fighting in the house. Tattoos are common now and parents need not run screaming out of the house that they have lost their child to the far side. Just say no and tell them eighteen is the age where they can make their own adult decisions. That's why there is a need for parenting, as the teenager still has a way to go before autonomy ensues.

Now for the boys. Most parents will admit that raising boys is easier emotionally than raising girls. Not to say they are a piece of cake. The family must accommodate the energy level and activity caused by elevated testosterone. The boys are trying to measure up for the task of competing for a place in the world. They must go against other males at every turn. So, they measure their dicks daily. They jump to see if they can touch the street sign. They punch one another in the arm to see who is stronger, and so on. They seek dominance and praise through sports. They contemplate a path to earning money while they struggle to keep erections in control, which can be a keen frustration in a seventh-grade class-room with the newly developed pretty girl seated at the next desk.

Boys must find a male role model to help them adjust, and unfortunately these days it's all about superheroes and video game violence. Most teenage boys are involved with sports. The lucky ones have it easier if they are in the nerd pack or the arts. They don't value the physical world of power like their sports-addicted classmates. They compare less, know they are different, and are fine with that. I can't tell you how many fathers I had to convince that their boys were normal even though they didn't sleep with a football.

Dads can be a great asset to their young teenager when it comes to lessons about sex and responsibility if they will only learn to talk to them. Telling your son about sex and mentioning his mother or sister in the same conversation is neither helpful nor wanted!

Boys generally are less concerned about feeling than they are on bottom-line decision-making. A boy will interrupt to ask what he should "do". He is more willing to learn by trial and error. Girls don't generally want to make mistakes and will talk and talk about it before reaching any decision.

Boys deal with more intense anger as that is the downside of testosterone and its effect on the body. It is a powerful drive coming from sexuality and aggression. It is primordial stuff, with the survival of the species at hand. If he is lackadaisical about mating, then everything might stop.

Boys must control their drives and learn to sublimate—and it sure helps if they can talk about it. They need a father who can communicate. Enter the therapist who helps Dad to do so. First, the father must be convinced that it is a good thing, even though some sporting event might be on tv. I ran men's groups in the past and the battle was always to get them to expand their two- or three-sentence summations. Women's groups had to learn to say it more concisely with less digressions.

With boys, it's about power and self-esteem matching up against competition, whether academic or sports or both. For girls, it's avoiding falling into the trap of relying on the physical, as that is what generations of women were taught. This attitude is evolving in present-day society. I recently watched a teenage girl pitcher strike out boys in a Little League tournament. When reporters interviewed her, she said she will make equal pay for what she does when she grows up. Not a gender issue, but an equality issue. Loved it.

The parenting of young teenagers is so important as they ask questions about what "it" is all about. Helping them refine and ask better questions and guide them through the decision-making process is what I have worked to do. Parents who learned to listen to their teenagers and not cut them off by giving advice before the issue had been fully heard was essential. "It" isn't easy, but it's necessary.

"It" Can Be Rough

We have seen that "it" can be your moment in the sun. It can be exhilarating and beautiful, as well as quiet and introspective. Depending on what you are looking for, it can be found anywhere at any time. To a therapist, "it" can mean secrets or events from the past that caused pain and suffering. Family secrets can affect not only the directly abused, but those in proximity as well. Unfortunately, there are more cases that fall into this category than is commonly known, except to the therapist community.

What is common are the coping patterns that families adopt. These coping mechanisms are why individual family members who have suffered abuse require treatment to overcome self-blame and enabling behaviors. It comes down to the abusers accepting responsibility and accountability for their behavior. In treatment, families learn to not be part of the problem, but part of the recovery. The most common and harmful response is to do or say nothing. The opposite is what is needed for recovery.

Let me give you an example made from a multitude of cases with the same issues. A large family came to treatment because one of the abused children, now an adult, had received individual help and now wanted to follow through on therapeutic protocol by involving all family members who were affected. Predictably, not all family members wanted to be part of treatment, or even talk about it. This was a religious family of seven children. The oldest three were girls, born one year apart—"Triplets", as the family referred to them. The boys were born eighteen months apart. The youngest girl was born one year later, followed by the youngest boy, born two years later. The exhausted mother had given birth to seven children in a little under ten years.

The father worked two jobs. The family followed a traditional pattern of a large, interactive, extended family with aunts, uncles, and cousins.

The problems began when the father's drinking became more habitual. He would come home late, drunk, after the children were in bed and would go and "check" on them. The oldest girl, who was about age nine, was uncomfortable with his "touching" her. She told no one. The behavior continued until she sealed herself in blankets to prevent the touching. The father then started on the next oldest. As is typical with this type of abuse, it is difficult to believe. This was a well-respected man in the community, although he did have a "drinker" reputation. The girls said nothing as they, like most victims, believed that they were somehow responsible for what was happening, as the father continually told them that he loved them while he was touching them. Not yet old enough to truly understand what was happening, they processed it as "he loves us".

As is also typical with this intrusive behavior, over the years it became buried in the girls' subconsciouses. The youngest girl also experienced the same behavior, but now the father was suffering from the effects of alcohol abuse and his memory was fragmented. His denial of the behavior was strong, which is common with alcoholism.

The children all had their own issues with alcohol and drugs, as young adults and adults. The oldest boy had severe A.D.D. and had issues with the law. The youngest girl was struggling with admitting she was gay. The middle girl had issues with depression and needed hospitalization twice. Everyone had difficulties with trust and relationships.

With families of alcoholics, there is a strong denial component. Who wants to admit that there is a family problem? It is more common to do everything to sweep it under the rug. That is what co-dependency is all about. People who covered for Dad thought they were keeping the family together. Also typical would be the wife's behavior of calling her husband's boss with some lie to cover for her husband's being too hungover to go to work. Other maternal behavior could be like hiding the bottles from the children and others, rather than dealing with the drinking directly. Its enabling behavior and it only fosters the continuation of the addiction. Treatment requires changes with consequences for actions detrimental for sobriety, and solid boundaries for people who are not addicted but live within the family system.

The alcoholism was a family problem because those who denied it in effect fostered it. Those who confronted it ran the risk of splitting the family into factions. It is very common to blame the healthiest person, who talks about the problem. They can be perceived as troublemakers "who should just stop talking about it".

Sexual abuse is even more difficult to admit or deal with, especially if the abuser takes no responsibility for his behavior and blames the accuser. Don't we see this played out every day in the newspapers, as men in power deny their behavior and blame the accuser? The "Me Too" movement deals with this every day.

When the oldest girl in the family finally figured out what had happened to her, she sought treatment at her husband's request. She uncovered all her childhood fears and memories and finally got the clear picture of why she was always nervous with sexual issues. She approached her next youngest sibling, who was still in denial. They became more distant as a result of these discussions. The mother was not much help as she defended the father, saying he was a "good man" and would "never do that". The two older boys also took this position. The oldest girl was encouraged by her original therapist to confront her father directly, after long and hard therapeutic preparation. When she did, his response was again predictable: he was offended by her accusation but told her he "loved her".

She wanted her siblings to understand what she had gone through, and what part they had played in enabling his alcoholism and subsequent sexual abuse. She was no longer hoping to get the father to accept his responsibility and get help, or even to apologize. She now understood his denial was central to his ability to function. He was not strong enough to face himself and what he had done. But she could now see that she had done nothing to cause his behavior.

After many sessions as well as reading and attendance at Al-Anon meetings, one of the sons admitted he thought his father could have done what the oldest daughter had accused him of, as she had no reason to make it up. Slowly, the family started to understand codependency and enabling as common conditions of what happens to children of alcoholics. They even started to notice it in their own behavior. The worst part of the disease is that it passes from one generation to the next.

The "it" here was the deep-seated feeling of anxiety that something was wrong. On a physical plane, it feels like a moving, internal gas bubble. It wants to come out, but it just keeps moving around, trapped in a circle. The same can be said for the entire family system. Something is wrong, but all attempts to fix it do not work and the problem remains. The truth is, the person who could help fix it is the one who caused it. Until he can stand hearing the truth, everyone else will suffer, one way or another.

If you look at families in recovery, they have taken responsibility for their thoughts, beliefs, and actions. They adopt new behaviors to realign responsibility and set consequences appropriately. No one can change the past, but they can do a lot to ensure it does not continue. There are at times hard choices that can and do include charging people with crimes.

The family in this case held a strong cultural belief that talking to outsiders about one's problems was wrong. This is common in most cultures. The Italians have two words for "wall", the outer wall which separates the house from the community, and the inner wall where nothing said inside that wall ever leaves the room. The secret is protected. The idea is not to air your dirty laundry. In doing so, the hierarchy of the family remains intact, and if it is led by a person who has power but takes no responsibility, the result is a fragmenting of the entire family. This Irish family had a long tradition of not facing problems and talking about it only caused more fighting, as no one was able to get to conflict resolution. Professional intervention was needed.

"It" is alive in so many families who suffer in silence with their secrets. It used to be homosexuality, which was treated as an evil and punished by societal norms. You could go to jail for whom you loved. Family members suffered shame and ostracization. Finally, as a result of the Pride Movement, we see the lessening of punitive attitudes as people no longer have to hide their secrets or blame themselves for what they feel. I look forward to the day that sexual abuse and alcohol/drug addiction is dealt with more openly by our society. Scandinavians do not punish offenders for what are considered disease behaviors. They do receive mandatory treatment, which is aimed at returning them to productive behavior. We in the USA are far behind in the way we deal with these difficult problems. "It" will continue until we educate and train our society to treat these disease conditions differently.

Sometimes You Just Get "It" Wrong

It happens quite often that people think they know what is going on, but they just get it wrong. They may get a piece of the story and they run with it. Other times, it's the premise that is wrong and the slippery slope begins. Good-intentioned people make bad decisions all the time. I remember one family who chased the story for months before they wound up in my office.

Mom, Dad, and their eighteen-year-old daughter came to me with a problem. Mom and Dad were a hard-working couple. He worked at the local manufacturing plant as a supervisor and Mom worked in a beauty salon. Neither one went to college and were very happy that their daughter, a B/C student, was advancing her education. She had attended college about two months when she started to complain to her parents that she didn't fit in and was having a lot of difficulty making friends. She was never a social person and had dated infrequently with marginal results. It seemed the boys never called her back. She was of average appearance and was a quiet, pleasant girl—more on the shy side.

The parents talked with her about making friends after class and possibly joining a club or two. "Sandy" replied she would try, but somehow the clubs met at inconvenient times for her. She was doing her assignments but was having issues with her English class professor after she wrote an essay about being alone in a school with classmates who had "hidden nastiness".

When the professor asked her to be more specific, Sandy became defensive and told the professor "it" would get worse if she talked about it. The professor dropped the issue, but there was now an awkwardness between them. The professor wanted to know more in order to help, but with this being an English class, there was nothing she could do if the student refused to elaborate.

The issue came to the parents' attention when Sandy said she wanted to drop the required English class but was prevented from doing so until she discussed it with the Department Chair. The Department Chairman felt it was an adjustment issue for Sandy and told her to work it out and talk to the professor.

Sandy told her parents that the professor had no right to "barge in" on her personal feelings and that what she had written about the other students was true. When I asked her to give some examples of the "hidden meanness", she described what she felt was kids looking down their noses at her. One girl had mocked her "high school" clothes and told her she needed a makeover. Other groups of female students "giggled" at her.

I thought this description sounded more like seventh grade than college. Right on cue, Mom said Sandy had a terrible time in middle school as she was shy, thin, a bit underdeveloped and often a target for the "in crowd" girls. Sandy said she wanted to do well in college and thought the Department Chairman must not like her. The parents were very protective and felt he could have been more understanding and helpful.

Sandy was having other issues as well, as she thought some of the kids were playing pranks on her. She swore that the kids had moved her car one row over in the college parking lot. She did not know how they could have done it, but she swore she had parked closer to the light pole. She also said that, after she had returned to the lunchroom from going to the bathroom, she noticed a few bites had been taken from her plate.

Sandy was becoming more resistant to going to college and was having stomach issues. Her parents took her to the family doctor and he felt she was having some adjustment issues similar to many other college freshman. Sandy said her stomach issues were real and had nothing to do with adjustment. She was told to take antacids.

After two more sessions, Sandy asked to have a session with just me, no parents. This was my plan, but I did not want to signal to her that I thought there was anything wrong with her, which would be suggested by my asking to see her alone. If she sensed that, she would never tell me what was really going on. Timing and trust are always key in therapy. Happily, she had made the offer.

During her individual session, she revealed that the college kids were now upping their game against her. She said the students were doing more severe things to her car when she parked in the lot. She had noticed little brownish dots on her car's trunk. "Why would anyone want to mess up that old piece of junk, anyway?" she asked. She said the car was fifteen years old and that the paint was worn in several places.

Sandy told me she had told her parents about it and they felt they should go to the police and file a report. She refused and the parents dropped the issue. She decided to announce outside class that she knew what was going on and that she would report anyone who continued to mess with her car. She began eating in a corner of the cafeteria so no one would touch her food. The parents felt she was being targeted because she wore the wrong clothes and the students were "college cliquey". Sandy said, "College is about individuality and this is mine."

During the next session, Sandy told me the spots were getting bigger and she was thinking of taking the bus to college and not risking more damage to the car. I spoke to her father and asked what he thought about her statements about the car. His response was that college kids play pranks all the time and the car was a piece of junk anyway and he wasn't concerned. He said he had never looked at the car, and I asked him to please check it out.

Sandy was having difficulty sleeping and was keeping her parents awake with her late-night complaints about nasty classmates. She could not understand why they were so mean to her as she barely knew them and they certainly did not know her. Dad kept promising to check out the car but never got around to it. I asked Sandy one day if she had brought the car to the session and she had. I asked if it would be alright if she showed me the damage that was being done to her car. "Gladly," she said, saying that the spots were even bigger now.

In summary, I had a family who was blind to the mental health issues of their daughter. Wanting to be supportive and helpful, the parents accepted her proclamations as factual. They sided with her on every issue. The problem was mean students and unsympathetic professors and administrators. They felt she was a fragile child and if they confronted her, they would run the risk of alienating her. Nice idea, but bad parenting.

The spots were simply rust on a very old vehicle. Anyone who saw her measuring the spots on the car would likely think she was weird. She was in the first stages of a paranoid delusion, and after some difficult persuasion I convinced her parents that she needed medication. Within a month, she was clear-thinking and was put in the hospital day program to learn some social skills. She completed the program and went back to school the following semester. Dad decided to junk the car and replaced it with one with a full coat of paint.

Sometimes, you just get "it" wrong.

Lessons from the Road

In order to sit in the therapist's chair, you must have a lot of life experience. The stories you will hear about people's lives and the decisions that they made will affect you in every way. Depending on the extent of your own exposure to the wider world, as well as your own capacity to understand, the sum of all that experience and knowledge will determine what you choose to focus on and how and when to intervene.

The two basic tenets of therapy, understanding and change, are the cornerstones of any therapy. Choosing the issue to address is what makes the difference in therapists. Young therapists are prone to jump on the first issue they understand about a patient. More seasoned therapists wait until the pattern reveals itself to the patient before making a comment.

The more you know about life, the deeper your compassion will be. When you said "I see" at age thirty, that was very different than the "I see" said at age sixty. The issues of class and social difference can best be narrowed by experience gained from direct exposure. It is difficult to understand poverty from the outside in comfortable surroundings, and very easy from the perspective of the person receiving the semi-monthly welfare check. You don't have to ride with the long-hauler who drives coast to coast to understand how he feels when he says he misses raising his kids; or, come from a single-parent household to empathize with a kid who didn't have a father at home. The goal is to have empathy for both sides and create compassion through understanding. You could gather the info from books or movies, but there is no substitute for real-life, one-on-one experience.

Fathers who worked in the mines and got sick didn't do it because it was a great job; it could have been that it was all they knew how to do, and the family relied on them. Mothers who sold drugs or turned tricks didn't do it because they were bad or liked the work. A lot of the time, it was due to limited choices or necessary opportunity.

Compassion takes longer to learn because you have to get past judgment. The adage of walking in someone else's shoes before making a judgment is true. We are all capable of violence, if the conditions make it so. You will do anything to me at some point if I try to cut off your air.

Not everyone will have had my experience of hitchhiking twice round trip, from New York to California. But the experience taught me so many lessons. Salesmen, truckers, farmers, waitresses, gamblers, cowboys, rural country folk, Texas Rangers, Scouts, pool hustlers, drinkers, beauticians, grocery store clerks, nuns, nursery school teachers, women prison guards, go-go dancers, lawyers, bouncers, country "fixers", and miners are some of the people who deepened my understanding of vastly different life styles. Nurses, teachers, and bus drivers all gave their opinions of the good life. Soldiers, hairdressers, and real estate agents all said their views on life and people were unique. Nurses and massage parlor workers all saw the best and worst in people. Talk to a doorman, bartender, office secretary, or a detective if you want to know what's going on with people. My favorite were the late-night diner waitresses, who had a base line perspective derived from years of conversations with everyone about everything.

Finding the common denominator in all people was what excited me. Boil it all down and people generally want the same thing, with age being the telling factor in what one wants. Young people want to expand, see and do it all, while they are still young; old people want only what they like. In the middle is where it gets tricky: old enough to know better, but young enough to still want to give it a go.

I liked hearing how the rich talked about the poor and how the poor talked about the rich. Very few of them had seen it from both sides. Prejudice permits you to talk about people you don't know or understand; you have a very definite opinion—until you actually meet those people and talk.

I grew up in a neighborhood that saw the 1960 Cuban migration. The locals were ignorant about who their new neighbors were. They viewed them as dirty, lacking values, and not to be trusted. Little did they understand that they were very similar in their values. The language difference was a barrier. It took years to understand that these Cubans were middle-class, former property owners, teachers, and businesspeople who had lost their homes and businesses to Castro. They were in the US to start over, in a country of mixed heritages. A little more than half a century later, one sees the prosperous Cuban community living here harmoniously with a thriving economy. The bicultural community is something we should all experience: the *medianoches* and *cafés con leche* are outstanding, and music is everywhere. The Cubans are now the landlords.

If you are open to seeing and understanding the other side, then you are open to change, and that will make you a better person and a better therapist.

There were so many times on the road that I had extended conversations with people who just wanted somebody to listen to their story. Outside Kansas City was a man who ran a tiny Mom-and-Pop store, but Mom was now gone. He was the conduit for town gossip, as everyone stopped in to tell him the local news or find out about who had just moved in. His philosophy was simple: "Do it right, and everything else will follow. Had me a good woman for fifty years and this store supplied it all. Kids came and went, health came and went, and my love came and went. But you know what? I am not sad or angry. All a man needs is what he needs, if he doesn't need it all. I filled a life with what I needed, and I got more than my fair share. Hope you get what you need, son."

A conversation like that can stay in your head forever, and the application of his life theory made for many meaningful therapy conversations.

I met a gypsy woman in New Mexico, who stopped in her tracks on the street and looked deeply into my eyes for what seemed like forever. "I know you," she said. "Not personally, but I know your tribe. It's your aura—it's unique and exists only in Eastern

Austria and Romania. Your family is from red-headed Jews. They were probably farmers."

She was one hundred percent dead-on. It was one of those moments when someone shows you something and you have no idea how they knew it. I couldn't speak. I just nodded to her. She walked away. So, what do you do with that experience? You spend a lifetime trying to look deeper and see where it came from. Isn't that what therapists do?

I was in Oklahoma City on a lazy, sunny afternoon, and I thought a bike ride would be nice. When I picked out the bike I wanted, the shop owner wrote down "1:30" and said, "Enjoy your ride." I looked at him a bit shocked, because he had not asked for any identification or a deposit. "Don't need it," he reassured me.

"How do you know I won't take the bike?"

"People around here don't steal bikes."

"I am not from around here."

"Ok, where would you go on that bike that I couldn't find you if I wanted to?"

It was so refreshing to be back in the land of basic trust. He assumed I would not steal, as that was his norm. Coming from New York, everyone assumes the other guy will steal. Its best to find out someone's norm before you assume anything about them. It's ironic that therapists generally make patients pay upfront before they teach them about integrity and trust.

I was stuck in the West Texas Panhandle, in a slim-pickings town called Odessa, with a broken manifold pipe in a car I was driving to Phoenix. It was late Friday afternoon, and the garage man said he'd have to order the pipe and it would be there probably Monday, Tuesday at the latest. I told him I had to have the car in Phoenix by Monday and asked him if he could build a pipe for me out of the scrap he had. He told me it would take a lot of welding and it would cost me. No guarantees. "Come back Saturday morning and we'll see what we can do."

So, I found a local beer and burger joint to get something to eat and pass some time. I would be sleeping in the car. I told my tale to a few men at the bar, who started laughing. "You asked Lem to build you a tailpipe? He couldn't put a screw in a nut if you gave him all day. Listen, kid. Go three blocks down and turn left for two blocks, there's a muffler place that'd still be open, and tell Larry Jimmy sent you."

Larry had the pipe, installed it in twenty minutes and I was on my way to Phoenix. Before I left, I stopped by Lem's and asked why he didn't tell me about the muffler place. "Well, you never asked." Lesson: Ask first before you go fixing things.

I was riding a horse on a two-day excursion with a scout in western Montana in Gallatin National Forrest. I was far from an experienced rider, but it wasn't my first time in the saddle, either. I followed the scout as we went deeper and deeper into the forest. I saw some amazing sights with all the animals that lived there. We came upon something that made the scout stop dead in his tracks. He turned and signaled to be quiet. He pointed to a clump of brush about twenty yards ahead: a baby moose was chomping away on some plants.

He whispered that the mother and father wouldn't be far away, and if they sensed the baby was in danger, they would charge.

Sure enough, the mother appeared, followed by the gigantic, large-antlered father. The scout said, "Don't move." I couldn't if I wanted to. He gestured to back my horse up easily. My mind went blank. *Where the hell is the reverse? I only know go ahead and stop.* After seeing me frozen and the horse not moving, he gestured for me to watch him. He gently pulled down and back on the reins and the horse started backing up. I am thinking, *If I get this wrong and the horse goes forward, I will be in deep shit!* I pulled down and back on the reins and nothing happened. I looked at him. He indicated I should do it a bit more forcefully. Ok, I tried it again—this time with a bit more elbow grease. My horse backed up until we were far enough away to turn around and get out of there.

When you are deep in the woods, real or symbolic, and you don't know what the hell you are doing, make sure you have someone with you who does.

Waitin' for the Last Dance

I was hitching and was about half-way between Little Rock, Arkansas and Memphis, Tennessee along Route 70 when I stopped in Brinkley, a small community in the middle of vast acres of farmland. This was the kind of town where time passed slowly. The people talked slowly, walked slowly, and they drove around town *very* slowly. Outside the general store was a wooden porch with a few rocking chairs. I got a coffee and a sandwich and sat down to watch what was going on. First impression was absolutely *nothing* was going on. A car slowly passed by, then a truck. A kid on a bike said "Howdy" to me as he walked into the store, his shopping list in his hand. A pickup truck that had seen better days rolled up and an older man with a badly bent cowboy hat got out and ambled up the stairs. He greeted me with "How do" and walked into the store. After he exited and put his packages in the truck, he came back to the porch and sat down next to me with his coffee.

He looked me over pretty good but didn't say anything. After a while, he looked over at me again and this time he said his name was Barney and asked me for mine.

"Tell you what I think", he started out. "Let's see if I can tell you about you and you tell me about me. It's a way to get some talkin' goin', if ya want to."

Sounded like a great idea to me. "Who goes first?" I asked.

"I will," Barney replied, "being I done brought it up. Ok, let's see, I don't see a car, so you got here with some help. You only have that knapsack, so you are traveling light. Probably hitching, because no one really comes here unless they have family or business. You are young and in good shape, so someone is feeding you well. You look pretty smart, so I am guessing you might be a college kid."

I smiled.

"You see, right there, that's a tell. You smiled, so it means I am on the right track. I am guessin' by your clothes, which don't have any dirt on them, that you are from pretty far from here. So, I'm a-thinkin', why would that young man be sitting here on this porch in this long forgotten town? Well, my guess is you are either going to Little Rock or you just came from there. You are having your lunch and then you'll be lookin' for another ride. So far, I think I am correct."

I smiled again.

"Ok, now let's see what you got to say."

"Ok," I replied. "Do I answer what you asked, or do I just do what you did?"

"You tell me about me."

"You came here in an old pick-up truck," I began, "and it looks like it's used for everyday chores. You have dirt on the tires and there is equipment in the back, so this is your everyday truck. You are dressed like a farmer and those mud-stained work boots indicate you probably have animals on the farm—either pigs or cattle or both. Your arms look very strong and your hands are calloused with scars, so you are working with them daily. Your hat has dirty finger marks on it, so you probably wear it while working, which means you are outside. So, you are a local cattle or pig farmer who likes to come to town and talk to anybody new as a form of entertainment."

He smiled. "Ha! A tell."

We both laughed and spent the next hour or so talking about life, people, and his philosophy about both. This was exactly why I wanted to hitch this country, to talk to the Barneys of America. He was born and raised in Brinkley and his farm had been in the family for three generations. His family originally came from Germany. They settled there and used their money to buy some land. When it became profitable, they bought more land and Barney now had 175 acres. He had been married for thirty-eight years and had five children. Two still lived on the property and worked the farm.

I told him I didn't have much of a story yet, as I had just graduated college and was on an adventure before I had to get a steady job in my home of New York City.

"Big city kid! Wow, we don't get many of them here."

I told him I was on my way back, as I had been to the North country and the West Coast and was now on the last legs of the return trip, with Memphis as my next stop.

"Well," he said, "you are having an adventure that all young men should have, and it will help you see the world a different way."

Barney went on the explain his philosophy and what he learned from living what he called "the good life". "Most people are impatient," he said. "They want things right away, and if it isn't working to their satisfaction, they either quit and move on or just become a miserable grumbler—and that is just plain wrong. They never bother to think that they might work harder and realize it takes more time to achieve anything worthwhile."

Barney spoke of his oldest son, who quit the farm about five times seeking other quick-paying jobs, only to return to the farm saying the road to success wasn't that easy "out there". He told me of his daughter who had been married three times with four children, and that she "marries in a hurry and then sees it isn't right for her, and she is like her father in that she listens to herself and has a tough time taking advice."

Barney told me it was a life task to figure out whom you should listen to and take advice from. Everyone needs to learn life's lessons, and those who do will fare better earlier and live happier longer. I asked him if he had any life lessons he could impart.

"Well, a lot of my lessons come from living here in this very small-town lifestyle. I don't know how that will apply to you all city folk. It's about waitin' for the last dance. That means, if you are in a rush—that could be for love or success or damn near anything you want—and you take what comes with the first dance, then you will never have to learn how to evaluate or choose among slightly different people or jobs. You may pass up something good, but you will only learn that once you pass it up. Hopefully, you have learned something."

He spoke of his wife, whom he chose after dating just about everyone around for miles. People thought of him as "Barney Bouncer" because he bounced from one woman to another. He said he endured all the chuckles because, when the last dance came, there she was and thirty-eight years later they were still right for one another. He summed up by saying, "You can't find 'it' when you demand it or want it—you have to wait and recognize it when you see it."

Sound words from a guy who knew "it" and found "it".

Linda and the Caddies

Sometimes you can learn "it" just by watching. I was in California as part of a West Coast trip and and I was visiting a friend of a friend. As it turned out there was no space available, but he said his neighbor across the street might have room for a few days. I was warned that "Linda", didn't always have "it" together, as she had a wild history of nutty relationships and several battles with "substances". I wasn't expecting this to be a "normal" visit.

Linda was very friendly and welcoming. She lived in a three-bedroom expanded cottage, which appeared no different from her neighbors. It had a garage under the first floor and a big deck out back. I met Linda's boyfriend, a man about twenty years older than she. They started drinking rather heavily right away.

They were a fun couple with very interesting and funny stories about the California lifestyle. According to them, the life there was about two reds. One was a bottle (wine) and the other was a pill (Quaalude). The goal was to stay high, not work, and let California's liberal support system pick up the tab. There wasn't much to admire about what I was hearing. But I was just passing through—and I did enjoy the wine.

Dinner the first night was predictable: a chaotic event which eventually became a phone call to a local taco joint. Linda couldn't find her wallet. I was introduced to two preppy-looking young men who were crashing at the house also. They were caddies with the PGA who traveled with the professional golfers. It seemed like an odd paring, but they liked the free room and brought their own drinks: scotch and bourbon. No one even mentioned how this arrangement came about.

Linda announced that she would be sleeping on her boyfriend's boat and would see us in the morning. I thought that a bit odd, as I was an unknown, but everything seemed a little odd there. I was given a room and, other than the caddies partying with some women and keeping me up well beyond my East coast bedtime, it was fine.

Linda never showed in the morning and the caddies left for the day. The refrigerator had a few jars of olives and pickles, and peanut butter and jelly seemed to be the standard. I went out for breakfast and toured around beautiful San Diego, then returned in the late afternoon to find the caddies on the deck cooking hamburgers. I called Linda, who said she was out of it and needed to sleep.

In summary, I visited a woman who rented a house but didn't live in it, at least at the time, and who had two men, now three, that she didn't know, living there. Either California had a code of trust that was beyond my grasp, or this looked like a whole heap of trouble. By the third day, Linda showed up and said she was going with her boyfriend to LA for a day or two, but I was welcome to stay. She would never have made hostess of the year.

I went to Mission Beach the next day and had a fine beach day. When I got back to the house, the garage door was open, and the garage was full of people looking over household items and buying them. The caddies were there, taking the money. They tried to tell me that they were helping Linda with her garage sale. These two had put up signs all over the neighborhood and were selling her stuff. Sometimes, you can't even believe "it" when you see it with your own eyes. I did call Linda and explain to her what I had seen. She said, "Oh well, probably didn't need any of that shit anyway." Just another day in the life when you have lost "it".

Colorado, then Montana

When I first saw them, they took my breath away. After hitching four hundred miles across interminably flat, boring Kansas, my entrance to Colorado was not much different—at least for the first hundred miles. Then, it happened: my first view of the Rockies. They continued to rise until they were in full view, on the other side of Denver. Powerful, majestic, mysterious, and magical, they stood strong against time. The mountains had an eerily connective effect on me, like I had experienced them before somehow, and we were reuniting.

My ability to process what I was seeing was limited by my Eastern background. My first night in the Rockies was spent sitting outside and peering into the star-filled sky. Although the day had been in the upper 80s, the cool chill of the night air was both confusing and welcoming at the same time.

My thoughts raced as I wondered if people ever got used to living among these pillars of time. Seeing the trails that wound their way up the sides of mountains before they disappeared made me think of the history required to make that path. *Who made them? Where are those people now? Are those Indian trails?*

My first morning in the Rockies, I saw nothing, as the view was completely covered in fog. When the fog finally lifted, it revealed a colorful combination of trees, orange dirt, multi-colored flowers and rocks, and a sky reflected in a deep, blue lake. The cool, morning temperature was immediately replaced with increasing heat. I exchanged my jacket for a t-shirt.

As I continued my journey west, the day seemed to change about five times, as one weather system after another blew in overhead. From clear to cloudy to clear again, then cloudy with rain and then clear once more. The mountains seemed indecisive about what they wanted to wear. I was fascinated by the size of these rocks and their constant change. What a beautiful place to live!

The small, fifteen-seat cafe was my chance to talk with the locals, who arrived in trucks of all sizes. "Mac" was a big guy with a beard who was friendly and willing to tell me about Colorado. He was a lineman for the power company. He said he was always busy, as the trees and wires "are not friends". I wanted to know about what it was like to live in those mountains. Mac looked at me hard for a second for two before he answered. Sensing I was serious, he told me the mountains dominated everything, from the weather to road conditions. In winter, he said, the mountains could be brutal and at times impossible. They created fierce winds and drove snow into blinding, white squalls that resulted in drifts of twenty feet or more. If rain mixed with the snow and the roads froze, travel was out of the question for days. In the spring, when the snow melted, the roads would flood and then his workdays lasted eighteen hours or more.

Mac then paused, saying that life was nonetheless good in the mountains because of their beauty and serenity. I was starting to understand that the "it" in these mountains was as complex as "it" gets. "These mountains," Mac went on, "have a history, and it's both good and bad, because they can kill you in a second or give you pleasure for years."

That was exactly what I was feeling: danger amid all the beauty. The steep slopes and downhill curves were dangerous in good, clear weather. What if you were driving and the weather changed quickly? The rivers that ran through the mountains changed rapidly as well. They went from trickles to rapids in a short time. I witnessed everything from peaceful scenes of children playing among the rocks at the water's edge, to pontoon rafts with racers wearing helmets and rubber suits.

The feelings that resulted were awe and excitement. Talking with Mac was wonderful, as he helped me to both love and respect the terrifying beauty around me. Growing up, I had felt the same about the Atlantic Ocean. I loved surfing, but I also had to respect water's power and the dangers of rip currents and rising waves.

Mac told me about the skiers who came to Colorado in the winter to ski Vail and Telluride, known for the best conditions for deep, long-range skiing. We talked for an hour and I was left with a feeling that there was a special "it" there in the mountains—if you were born there, it was in your blood.

Continuing my journey, I headed to Wyoming and then into southwest Montana. If I thought Colorado had "it" with the Rockies, then it was a whole new game in Montana. Paradise Valley is an aptly named stretch of land that goes from Livingston, Montana south to Yellowstone Park. The Yellowstone River runs along the valley to Gardner at the beginning of the park. If you ever want a fifty-mile raft ride, then you have found your spot.

This tract of land was one of the most beautiful I had ever seen, with the breathtaking Gallatin Range of mountains to the west, and the greenest, most fertile soil for farming. The Big Sky ski resort, built by Chet Huntley, was at the southern end of the valley.

Montana's weather is like Colorado's, but a bit more challenging. It can range fifty degrees in one day. Locals told me that they use electric blankets to keep their car batteries from freezing in winter. No one can drive anywhere unless they have a sturdy, four-wheel drive vehicle with BIG tires. The summer is their time to shine, as the weather is hot, but calm—unlike the fierce thunderstorms they have in the spring and fall. Like Colorado, the story is the mountains. From my cabin in the woods, I could hear the howling of the wolves. That eerily beautiful sound made me feel I was experiencing life beyond what I could see. The *whooshing* sounds as animals raced past was what made "it" so special.

The Montana sky seemed to go on forever. I could see different weather systems approaching—not like New York, where I had limited visibility of anything more than an hour away. In Montana, you can see five hours away, depending on wind speed.

I was never the same after I saw Montana, as there was a beauty beyond what I knew. I had lived with skyscrapers but not the sky. The challenges of New York were traffic and congestion.

In Montana, space was endless, and time was slower. I found an "it" there that has stayed with me ever since the first day I saw the mountains. I can watch movies of them and still "feel" them. The "it" is a combination of peacefulness and power, with an overriding feeling of eternity, as they will be there long after you and I are able to see them.

And Now for the Waitresses ...

There should be a book by itself to cover the exploits of these working warriors, but I will cite as many examples as I can. You will recognize them, as they are part of the fabric of the American diner experience. But first, let's look at some of the different types of diners. I'm not talking about their design, which is another book, but mainly about their locations and their clientele. Here's the short list:

We will start with the local diner, the one in town that serves families and day workers. Usually a jolly, busy place—a Greek is not far away. Next is the diner with the short counter, sometimes referred to as a "greasy spoon". Then there's the late-night diner, where you'll find the third-shift, industrial folks; the country diner, which is never open at night; the standard, roadside diner that serves weary sojourners; the truck stop diner, huge parking area for big rigs, more of a department store that serves food cafeteria-style. There is also the bar/diner combination—almost a restaurant, with a "better section" that serves alcohol. A lot of these categories overlap, but they will get us on our way.

Now, for the waitresses. The local diner has a family, mom-type waitress. She knows the customers and they know her. She will call you by your name and is uniformly friendly (no pun intended). Conversations here are not long, as the place is busy. You wait in line at high traffic times. If you ask her, she'll tell you everything on the menu is good. There are usually younger waitresses during after-school hours, and they make a face when you mention some food they don't like. People have been coming to the place for years for its list of specials. Mom will tell you the one that is most popular.

Breakfasts and lunches are packed with customers. Dinner is quieter. If you want to have a conversation with the waitress, the best time is after the dinner hour, at closing. Mom has left and the second shift is tired. This is when they dish out the gossip or "town dirt". The waitress will tell you that she "can't say for sure", but she has heard … and at the end of her story she'll remind you that you "didn't hear it from me". Elections are won and lost in these diners. Town secrets get exposed—they know who is a shoddy contractor and which lawyer you should get. The conversations between the local waitress and the local female real estate agent are ones you should never miss—they know the town and how their customers really live.

One subject you can always talk with them is sports. Either their father, husband, brother, sister, son or daughter has played on the local team or coaches one. The overall feeling with her is one of warmth. Mom also makes sure that no one gets out of line. It's bad for business.

Julie was one of the "Mom" types. I was seated at the counter in a diner in Birmingham, Alabama when I asked her if she had any sort of philosophy on running the diner and dealing with the general public. She smiled and said, "Don't say what you're thinking." Then she added, "Well, I spend a lot of time here, and I want to make it as enjoyable as I can for myself. If I do that, then the diner will be happy as well. As for the customers, they come in all types, and if you are smiling and friendly and serve them what they want, they won't cause any tension." I asked her if that was possible and she replied, "Of course. Just remember to not say what you are thinking."

The "greasy spoon" diner caters to quick-service foods. The cook makes all the food in front of you behind the counter. This is your basic, dirty t-shirt guy, covered with the day's food stains. He might have on a soiled apron as well. The waitress here is not as friendly. She's mostly business. She will nod at you for your order. She looks unhappy, as if she is saying, "Look where the hell I wound up—and don't ask." The clientele here are not looking for fancy; they just want to fill up. The title "greasy spoon" is derived from two sources: the amount of oil on the grill, and the "quick dip" cleaning of the silverware.

If you want information from this waitress, you'll need to go outside and catch her on a cigarette break. She will be curt and eye you with a timer ticking. She knows a lot of stuff from listening to conversations, and most of it she doesn't like.

The "greasy spoon'" at night feels more like the "Last Chance Saloon." Clientele has dropped a notch or two from the daytime, and the night waitress always wears too much makeup. It is a big contrast to find someone with bright, indelible red lipstick working in these rather glum, drab establishments. The lipstick is her last defense against feeling invisible.

My favorite "waitress look" is the long stare, with eyelids half-closed, that she gives the guy at the counter when he can't make up his mind about what to order. If she's had a rougher night than usual, she might just say "Order the f-in' hamburger! We don't have all night!"

Why do people go here? The price is usually good and there are few alternatives.

I caught Marianne, a young woman in her early twenties, on her break outside the "spoon" in Scranton, Pennsylvania. I told her I was writing a book and she looked to me like she would have something interesting to say about her job. She smirked. "Really?" she said. "First of all, don't work here." When I laughed, she replied in all seriousness "No. I mean it. It's not good for you." I asked why, and she responded, "Because of the assholes and losers that come in every night looking for something they'll never have." When I asked her what that was, she said, "A woman to take care of them, a normal conversation, and a life beyond desperation." "Pretty heavy stuff," I said. "Look around!" Marianne said. "This was a coal town and the mines closed sixty years ago! This place has been f'n depressed ever since, and these dumbasses are too lazy to move." I looked at her for a moment. "How do you survive it?" I asked. "Me? I watched my mother go down the tubes with this life, and it's not going to happen to me. I am saving every dime I make to get the hell away from here." "And do what?" I asked. "Doesn't matter! I just want to talk to people who think tomorrow will be better and wherever that is, I will find it." I wished her luck and told her I hoped she found her peace. "Where do you live?" she asked. I asked her why she wanted to know, and she said, "Well, in just a few minutes with you, I had a normal conversation. Maybe there are more like you there."

I thanked her for the compliment and later went out for breakfast with her when her shift was over. I gave her my address and we wrote to one another for years. She wound up in Texas, married with three kids and running a bed and breakfast. Her last letter to me was funny. She said she was happy and the house where she lived has so much land "that you can't see an asshole for miles and miles".

The late-night diner waitress is the real deal. There was one of these diners in New York's meat packing district that served men and women working in the meat processing plants. They go to the diner on their breaks, wearing their bloody aprons. It is quite a sight. Their shifts end at three or four in the morning and they return to the diner for breakfast.

Over the years, the place had added a small stage in the corner with a dance pole. They hired dancers, and the waitress herself showed lots of cleavage.

She would bounce behind the counter from one bloody apron to the next, slinging eggs and hash browns. She did not appreciate the dancers, as they took away from her being the center of attention. But it was good financially, as the dancers brought in the customers.

It was nearly impossible to talk to her, as she was very busy. You had to catch her between meat house breaks, before the dancers showed up. There are usually two types of waitresses in this type of establishment. The first is the pretty young girl trying to make tips who thinks it's cool to work there. Her friends think she's nuts, but she is an adventurous sort and the job is good experience. The other end of the spectrum is the fifty-plus woman who has seen it all and this place doesn't faze her. She wears heavy make-up and her blouse is more open than it should be, probably as *de riguer* for tips in this "testosterone palace". She will call you "hon".

Is there any "it" here? Of course—it's basic. These women see the primal man all the time, and if the place is crazy enough to get a liquor license, the talk gets more sexualized because of the alcohol/testosterone combination—and because of *that*, the waitresses make good tips.

I asked a waitress named Alice what men are all about. "Well, they have one hand on their dick, the other on their fork, and their problem is deciding which one to drop when they want to drink." That, friends, is "it".

Other more standard late-night diners include the ones generally advertised as "Open 24hrs". These can be urban, suburban, or open road. The late-night experience here is varied, but the waitresses are older and it's not their first shift.

The urban, late-nighter waitress has seen it all. She handles all problems quickly and her language is salty. The crowd is the urban spectrum, from people just getting out of bad weather, to people who have no other place to go. A common reason as to why she works here can be, "my husband works days"—and then she grins. She knows that local bar crowd, as the place fills up when the bars close. She has little tolerance for them and is quick to remind them that "86"—the universal term for those about to be thrown out—applies in this establishment as well.

If you can speak "waitress", she will talk to you. That means you understand that working with the general public can be exhausting. This is the "key" to connecting with her: you have to shake your head when she does, smile at her approvingly, and your comments should let her know she's got your support for all she has to put up with. If you can pass through her screening system, she will talk to you.

She has a wealth of information on the state of the human condition. As a therapist, my best conversations could be with her. I always thought the "waitress interview" should be a required college course. To pass the course, you must be able to engage her for twenty minutes.

I spoke to Vicki in a Minneapolis diner. She was nearly fifty, twice-divorced and had a boyfriend. "What's it take to work here?" I asked her. "God," she replied. "If you don't have somebody watching your back, this life will swallow you up—and that's coming from a fairly normal person. I have trained myself to think that something passed these people by, and I hope it comes their way again, so they can jump on it … this time."

Vicki was straight-forward, down to earth, and almost spiritual in her delivery. She had made her own share of poor decisions, but she remained upbeat and at the same time cautious.

"The minute you relax and think you have found 'it', she told me, "it will play a trick on you and go away." "Isn't that negative?" I asked. "No. It's just the way it is—you may have your head in the sky but keep your feet on the road. I have learned the hard way. People around here are good, honest and trusting, but that is where the devil plays. God is looking out for me, like good insurance." She laughed. "I think that qualifies as good 'it'."

The suburban, 24-hour, late-night diner waitress is the one who will talk to you. She is a working-class woman, working mainly with the middle class. "They have more of everything", according to Rachel, a waitress in the Atlanta suburbs. "But they are not happy." She overhears all the suburban cheaters and late-night couples who have someone else at home. These waitresses do not work in the towns where they live. It's like the AA crowd who goes two towns away for their meetings. Why do they do that? Because they don't want to be at a meeting with their neighbors.

If you are working the night shift, your skill set is basic. God bless these women, because this could be their second job. Theirs is usually a hard luck story of failed marriages and troubled kids. Rachel has very little life outside work, because there are financial responsibilities. She helps her daughter with the two kids and the absent father. She looks tired: the eyes give it all away. Her "it" is people aren't who they say they are. She sees it all the time, and in her drudgery from work to work to home to work, she isn't high on the good life. How could she be? She sees people with money who are miserable, and her own life is not far behind. It breaks down like this: if you are poor and the people you work with are poor, there is a commonality of the sharing of joy or misery. If you are poor and "they" are not, it sets up a competitive atmosphere. Ever notice how a middle-class person sometimes treats "the help"? Well, in the diner, it is right out in the open for all to see. "Get me a—" is a lot different from "May I please have …?" The reason Rachel is easy to talk to is that she has few opportunities for offloading. I found that women like Rachel also talk out loud to no one in particular. It can be very cultural. Rachel explained it: "Ever notice that white people won't start talking until they make eye contact? But black people will just start talking and then look around to see who is listening." Interesting observation. "Why do you talk to no one in particular?" I asked her. "Just to get it out— ain't easy being black."

You would think diner conversations in suburbia would be happier. They are not. Of course, this is not everyone, but if you get the chance, take a look-see for yourself. Rachel was a bit depressed, and it showed. I thought she had the first signs of burnout. I came by every night for four nights, as I wanted to see if she had an upside. She had seen too much. It was sad.

The "open road, 24-hour" diner is way different. This is mainly because the clientele is not local. They are on the road and have been alone in their cars, and the counter at the diner provides a social forum.

The waitress here has many stories to tell about the travelers they meet. What is interesting is that people are on different schedules. Some are eating dinner, while others are eating breakfast. Some have just gotten up and others are ready for bed.

Betty feels free in this environment, as there are no local, personal stories to be heard. I asked her outside Kansas City to tell me about the people there. She gave me the "Why?" look. "Because I am just passing through, and you know all these people," I said.

She jumped on it: "I don't know their names, but I do know their types. For example, that table of four in the corner—they are going to order hamburgers with fries and lots of soda. The nervous lady at the end table is going to have a house salad and ask me ten questions about it. The couple holding hands and talking will take forever to order—she'll remind him of his diet. The big guy at the counter is going to have the platter—with extra gravy."

I asked what I was going to order.

"By your Eastern New York or wherever accent and your body type, I bet you'll go for the chicken salad sandwich."

Damn, she's good. She's got "it".

Betty could also spot "trouble" in a second. "It's a feel you get, something is not right: they are either too nervous or too 'hidden'. People are very readable, and they signal all the time. You just have to learn how to read them."

Now for the truck stop diner. First, they are huge and cater to truckers—long-haulers, if you will. Men and women who drive the big rigs from coast to coast. The road warriors of America. In bygone days, they were on their CB radios talking to their "good buddies". They all had "handles" and there were a million country songs about them. These days big riggers have all the modern technology from GPS to live Instagram. But the culture of the road is still alive and well in these stops.

They often serve cafeteria style, where people can pick out their own food. There are still separate areas for "table service".

The waitresses here are used to being hit on. But, nowadays, there is a "special" service that can be purchased outside where the rigs are parked. That's where the trucker and the truck both get serviced.

The waitress here has a different view of marriage and family. Most of these truckers spend more time away from their families than with them. They say it's financial, but if you actually ride with them, they will tell you their only truly happy time is when they are on the road, with their music, their tv and radio, and their communication network. The rigs are big enough to offer a good-sized bed, a refrigerator, a microwave, and any other electric appliance one might want. When they hit the diner, it is to join in the camaraderie of kindred spirits.

Dotty sees married men who live single most of the time. Their view of relationships makes women seem like position players and not the starting team. The men are there and gone, and who is to say it doesn't work for them?

Dotty loves these guys as they are good to her. Her "stop" was a "76" outside Indianapolis. They flirt with her, kid around, and make a lot of noise. She knows the road culture and speaks their language. The drivers and the waitresses are very simpatico and the "it" here is a shared aloneness. If the route the men take is the same, they will pass by once every two weeks or so. "It's kind of a relationship, don't you think?" I asked her. Dotty agreed. "I even know the space between visits. I look forward to seeing them and talking. But, for me, the best part is that they hit the road when the meal is over. I like men, like spending time with them, and there sure are a lot of them. But I wouldn't want to take care of them. They're too needy and some are too controlling—they start telling you what you should or shouldn't do. The best ones put on their boots and leave when the deed is done, if you get my drift."

"I do," I replied. "No hanging around looking for more."

"Exactly," Dottie says, "but come back the next time."

Dotty has found "it".

The last stop is the diner/bar combo. This hybrid is becoming more and more popular. Generally, it has one side that's a simple diner, while the other side has linen tablecloths and comfortable booths. A bar separates the two. Depending on location, these hybrids can be very popular.

The waitress in this establishment can make more money due to higher bar tabs. Some patrons use it as a bar with side dishes. The owner likes to see the place full. There can be fierce competition to get the best section, according to Marlene, an experienced waitress in Northern New Jersey. "Once they put the bar in, everyone wanted to work here. Waitresses need tips and the bigger the bill, the bigger the tip." She said it has not made staff relations better. Although alcohol can be served on both sides, the diner crowd tends not to do the mixed drinks.

So, where does every waitress want to work? According to Marlene, the waitresses bicker among themselves, accusing some of getting preferential treatment when they are frequently scheduled on the bar side. "It made the place more tense," she says.

I asked her what it was like to work there compared to any other restaurant.

"I like diner people. They are straightforward and not fancy. They don't need a tablecloth or a plant nearby to eat. Those going to the 'better' section are kidding themselves. Same kitchen. Same bar. I don't get it. If they want that, then go to a different restaurant, but I think the reason this concept works is that it lifts some people up to eat on the 'better' side, and they can get it cheaper here than a real restaurant."

"Sounds like you don't have such a good opinion of your customers," I remark.

"To me," Marlene says, "any customer giving me a tip is a good customer, but I don't want people putting on airs. It annoys me when people come in and ask for the 'better' section. Listen, I've worked in diners for twenty-five years and honey, it ain't better over there. It's the same people who used to sit on the other side and liked it fine. Just don't try to seat some of these people on the diner side. I heard one woman say, 'Oh! That's not us'. Really? Well, let me tell you something, 'Miss Fancy Pants', your ass is still in a diner."

Marlene is perceptive and funny, with a string of one-liners learned from all her experience. She likes the younger crowd, whom she has had to educate about proper tipping, as they tend to stay longer and are notoriously bad tippers. But the kids provide fun and laughter—a good thing.

She summed up the hybrid experience like this: "Bottom line, it's more money, but like everything else in life, it comes with a price. It causes tension between the girls and the different managers really don't want to hear it. For me, I liked it the old way—less bullshit to deal with."

Street Lessons

I was working the Lower East Side of New York as a social worker. My territory included the Rutgers Houses, a rather rough welfare set of buildings, and the surrounding area of Henry, East Broadway, Madison and Monroe streets. There were three main groups of people occupying this settlement area of the city. Blacks lived to the East, Puerto Ricans lived mainly in the middle, and Chinese to the southwest. Most of the territorial street gang fights occurred where the areas intersected. I had the task of working the streets while trying to work with the Police Juvenile Division and the city's Department of Social Services. Our mission was to determine the issues and try to mitigate the violence. I worked well with each individual group, after a period of testing and trust-building. I was able to communicate well with the black and Puerto Rican gangs. The Chinese would not be seen talking to any white person, as they would lose status, and they were too busy fighting among themselves anyway. Meetings with them were always in secret: in a room downstairs, usually behind a restaurant kitchen. The issues were the same as they had been for generations. The old neighborhood resented the intrusion of the new people moving in. Originally, it was the Italians, Jews, Irish, Germans, and Poles, who had these territorial wars.

It took quite a while to build any trust, and when it came to negotiation of territorial disputes, a decision had to be made. If you were perceived to be on one side or the other, the talks stopped immediately and name-calling ensued. If you made no decision at all, you were perceived as weak and ineffective. The skill was to be the universal lawyer of all sides, representing their points of view in the prolonged battle for recognition. Reframing their words in a more universal context so that the others could swallow them was a recurring event at meetings—like in a family battle between moms and dads or kids and parents. I learned it was better to play the grandparent who could say anything about any side of the argument, because they were out of it anyway and had nothing to lose.

One of my favorite welfare buildings was way over on Delancey Street between Attorney and Ridge. It was about 80% black with some recent Hispanic arrivals. The two biggest days of the month were the fifteenth and the thirtieth—that's when the bi-weekly welfare checks arrived. My building was all females with children. During the day it was a female haven. Kids played in the streets, with lots of bicycles and ice cream trucks. The only men you saw were the delivery men and the mailman, and some social workers like me. At night, there were male visitors to the apartments. But on check day, multitudes of men arrived shortly after the mailman.

These were the "invisible" fathers and boyfriends. They offered to go shopping and "help". It was the loudest two days of the month, because all the women vented their anger at these men who never helped with the kids or did any sort of parenting. When the money arrived, they were all sweet talk and promises. Instead of showing up *with* money, they were looking *for* money. I would talk to the women about not giving away money they needed to men who were only "players". I knew the women would be calling me before the next check, looking for "emergency" funds. They fell for it time and time again. The men made up every excuse for why they needed the children's food money for themselves.

Finally, the women and I got together for a meeting and the resulting agreement was to include everyone together in the battle to keep their needed money. The first task was to make up a big poster board. We agreed to look at the board before every check arrived. On the left, we listed all the women, with a space for the date. In the next column were the men's initials or his street name. In the next column was what he said he needed the money for.

Seeing their lives in black and white had an effect on the young women, as they saw they were all being "played" with the same lame excuses over and over again. They had originally thought it was their fault and were too embarrassed to admit it. Seeing the excuses in a pattern helped them say no. They entitled the board "What Goes Around Comes Around".

Patterns only change when there is an awareness, along with some support from those around you. Not everyone was able to keep their word, as the men changed their tactics as well. We all learned that it was hard to change the flow of a river that goes where it wants.

Religious Teachings

The search for "it" is very powerful in formal religious teachings. Millions of people have been guided by its principles. Worship is a way of life for so many people. What is interesting is that the separate religions do not support one another. They become rivals and often go to war. My own experience with religion was rather brief and unrewarding. For me, I never found "it".

It's sad to say, but it's true: religion has a dark history. I know Christians preach "turn the other cheek", but they also justify wars with "God on our side". Some deem others as "infidels" and believe they should be killed. Muslims justify either Shia or Sunni to permit their tribal slaughters of one another. The Khans in Asia used their religious tribal beliefs to slaughter millions. Today, in Myanmar, the government permits the killing of Muslims in their northern territories. The Taliban in Afghanistan kills people because they don't follow their edicts, such as reading about other religions. The Russians and Chinese have committed "ethnic cleansing" forever. The English came to America and killed the "Godless" Indians. African tribes kill because their ancestors did.

I could go around the globe to make my point, but it's unnecessary. If you believe, fine. Believe. But you have no right to tell someone else how to believe or ultimately kill them for their beliefs. People today misunderstand ISIS as a war between Muslims and everyone else. Not true. These are terrorists who do not even understand the Muslim religion yet kill under that banner. True Muslims denounce them as fakirs.

Most people get spiritual guidance along with a sense of shared community. Religion also offers a belief system that prepares them for death. A road map for life, with rituals and ceremonies.

I had two religions in my family—well, four, actually—but no one practiced any of them. My mother called herself a "free thinker" with a kind of self-determination against a forced conformity. Her mother was Protestant and her father was Catholic. No one went to any church. My grandmother found a little church one block away from her apartment and spent some time trying to get my grandfather to go. He went once and conveniently got "dizzy" and never went back. He never got "dizzy" again, either. Grandmother never returned to the little church.

My father was an Orthodox Jew, and then to acculturate, he married my mother, the "shiksa". He got drummed out of the family for that unforgivable act. If you like family dynamics, then welcome to my home. Jewish and German Christian, with a last-minute declension on my mother's part to Agnosticism. Sounds like the local wrestling card. "Tonight, in the preliminaries, the Jew faces off against the Fraulein. The winner will meet the Agnostic. Come one, come all!" In my apartment, it was about power and control—not religion.

I heard my mother tell my father that neither the Jews nor the Christians were right, and they will never agree, but they shared one similarity: they both wanted your money.

My father never taught me anything religious, but he did educate me on the ways of the Jewish social community—mostly its food. I learned about Jewish delis as he took me to them all the time. Chopped liver on rye with a slice. Borscht with sour cream. Potato knishes. Dr. Brown's Celery Soda. Mile high pastrami sandwiches with mustard—never the dreaded mayo. He would say, "Jews eat dark. If you are ever given a choice, choose dark over white, especially with breads and meat." Chicken soup, a Jewish family specialty for anyone with a cold, got an asterisk along with whitefish.

My mother sent me to a Protestant church, although she never went. The minister was a nice guy, but their "be good" message got old after a while and I was already good. Those damn hymns they sang were neither musical nor spiritual—they were horrible. Nothing like the music I listened to. It had no melody whatsoever. A trip to a black, soulful church should be on their mandatory update list.

When my father died suddenly, this same minister came to the house to explain to me that my father would not go to the Christian heaven because he was neither baptized nor had "accepted Christ". This information stunned and shocked me. It left me cold and I felt totally unsupported in my time of extreme grief. If "they" didn't let in good people like my father, why would I spend a life following their beliefs in order to get to their heaven? Why would I want to go? Thanks, Rev Poole. You saved me a lot of amens and plate-passing.

I never set foot in a church after that day. All the pomp and glittery-gold ceremonial robes and stories about virgin births fell on my deaf ears. Christmas, Easter, and any other Christian holidays meant absolutely *nada* to me. I viewed them as false promises. My father was a good, kind, and caring man who always did the right thing because that was how a person was supposed to act, according to him. He was moral and taught me never to steal or take anything that wasn't mine. You want something, you work hard to get it. Bottom line for me was, if that Christian heaven place didn't want him, then it wasn't for me either. I always doubted there was a heaven place anyway, as when I learned science and took the Haydn Planetarium Space Voyage, there was no "warm spot" heaven in the freezing vastness of space.

So, what guided me? If I were going to accept that when I died it was all over, and religion was not going to be of any help, then I had to have some kind of life-philosophy or goal to reach before that day arrived. I found relief in Existentialism, which to me was a kind of *noir* belief that you made "it" what you needed it to be. If goodness was a virtue, be good. Same goes for kindness and caring. If things were bad, then don't do them.

Then there was this existential belief about boundaries. Basically, it said setting them correctly is your life's goal. If you set your life experience boundaries too narrowly, you will always feel a yearning that you could have done or been more. If you set them too wide, then you will always feel frustrated that you never accomplished what you set out to do. That's the "A-ha moment", right there.

Theatre of the Absurd appealed to me, for it was always putting its characters in this existential paradigm of doing too little or doing too much. Setting your correct boundaries permits you to search for meaning within a range, and it results in a higher degree of life satisfaction. My existential proclamation to myself at seventeen was to live life to the fullest, so that I would never have that deathbed "A-ha" moment where you sit up and realize you have never really lived at all.

I can say now at age seventy-eight that I have really lived and am at peace as I have accomplished my goal. I have seen the human experience in a vast array, I have traveled the world and, most importantly, due to my life's work as a healer/therapist, I have helped multitudes of people change their lives for their own betterment. There will always be more to see and do and hopefully I will continue this path to add more meaning. Having gone past my life expectancy, I am in "bonus time", and now my end focus is to use philanthropy to help those in need. I also want to help everyone find "it". Is that too big a boundary? I don't think so, and therefore, I am writing this book. The book can do my work when I am no longer here.

In retrospect, I am no fan of religion. I see it as a divider of people and, at its worst, a justification for war. Moral and ethical behaviors do not need a religious banner, but they do they need an awareness and a commitment. I say to students, "Your path is out there: find it and stay on it. We will all be better off because of you."

It Lives in the Night Court Gallery

Ever been? Night court in New York City is *really* at night. They should really call it Late Night Court. It's not your 7pm court for people with full time jobs who commute. This one is for all the people who don't fit into the daytime. The first rule of thumb is to remember that this is *not* the court of the TV character Judge Harry Stone from the 1980's series, *Night Court*. It's more like "Judge Judy's" court when she is pissed off at people who are not answering her questions.

The gallery at night court is where the action is. Mostly, its people waiting their turn in front of the judge. The side comments are amusing. It's is a very popular place to go for people who don't have a tv or just want free entertainment.

The door opens, and people in handcuffs who were just arrested get to be arraigned in front of the judge. It's mostly procedural stuff, but the charges get a good gallery response. Interspersed are the cases on the docket for that night.

It is common for writers to go, as the various forms of the human condition are on full display. One thing is for certain: you'll have no idea that people did the types of things these folks are accused of.

Before we begin, put yourself in the gallery and be prepared to treat it like it's a movie and you can talk to the screen—not too loudly, as it's still court, but no one really stops the banter as the judge has a mic. As long as he or she is heard, nothing else matters. Ready? Here we go …

A black guy in a street hustler suit with multi-colored pointy shoes comes in, smiling, his gold tooth showing prominently. The black women in the gallery are instantly animated. "Damn! This fool did whatever they say he did!"

The charges are read. The man is charged with stealing jewelry, resisting arrest, and contributing to unsafe public conduct while in possession of a concealed weapon (a knife). Doesn't sound all that bad, depending on how big that knife is. His girlfriend had seen him walking down the street with another woman and spotted her missing necklace dangling from the woman's neck. When she demanded he give it back to her, the guy told her some made-up story and a fight ensued among the three of them: pushing, shoving, slapping. Someone called the police and when they arrived, they found the guy trying to pry the necklace from the angry girlfriend's clutches. The scuffle resulted in him being arrested as the police saw him push the girlfriend to the ground.

The black women in the audience render their verdict: "You

can't be wanting a dude that stupid!" The black men in the audience respond: "But these bitches did!"

Meanwhile, the judge is pissed that he has to hear "this nonsense" and dismisses all charges. "Get these children out of my courtroom," he tells the bailiff.

Next, five Chinese men are brought in, all handcuffed to one another, their heads hanging. Murmurs in the gallery suggest the charge will have something to do with gambling. The five men are charged with running an illegal lottery in a Chinese restaurant. When they refused to pay the winner, accusing him of having a phony ticket, he called the police.

"These same guys were here last month," one guy in the gallery states. "The only reason they are here is that they probably missed the cops' payment, and the cops are tired of them."

Two flamboyantly gay guys are handcuffed together. They are wearing multicolored outfits usually associated with street prostitutes. They are charged with disturbing the peace and in possession of drug paraphernalia. The gallery murmurs "turf war". It's determined that the two had had a screaming match over who controlled a certain corner, and the owner of the nearby café was fed up with all the squabbling in front of his place. When he told them to find another spot, they turned up the volume and got the customers into the fray. When they wouldn't stop, the police were called.

The judge asks: "Is the whole night going to be like this?", to which the gallery applauds. (I like the gallery. They are quick and get right to it).

Two cops escort a huge, cuffed man wearing only a very large blanket and boots. His hair is styled in beaded cornrows. The gallery erupts with "Jamaican crazy". He is charged with being a public nuisance and threatening customers on the Circle Line, a tourist cruise around Manhattan. He had opened his blanket, exposing himself while demanding money from the riders. The gallery wonders who sold him the ticket to get on the boat. (I recognize the guy as a man who lives in the park at Sheridan Square). The judge orders Social Services to get him a pair of pants and a shirt and send him to Bellevue Psych for observation.

An attractive young woman and her equally attractive, well-dressed partner are brought in in handcuffs by a smiling cop. The gallery is slow to respond. Finally, someone says "What the hell are those two doing here?"

They are charged with public fornication. The gallery loves it as they muse over where the two might have been caught "doing it". It turns out they were having sex in the elevator of a high-end hotel. The doors, which they thought they had disabled, opened onto the hotel restaurant patrons.

The act is the result of a college wager. The gallery rolls their eyes and the judge tells them to "get a room".

Four tough looking, young Hispanic men are brought in by four cops. All have tattoos and stud jewelry. The gallery is divided over "gang shit" or "drugs". The men are charged with running a dog fighting operation in the basement of a bodega. "Didn't see that one coming," the gallery says.

An older man wearing an orange prison jumpsuit is brought in by a cop who is shaking his head. The gallery erupts in laughter. "This fool is already in the system. What's he doing here?" It appears the man was on an early release program, doing outside garbage pick-up, and he escaped. The cops were embarrassed and had brought him to court—after discovering him hiding in the park he had been cleaning.

The man faces charges for escape and the gallery empathizes that he was getting too close to his release time and he wanted to stay "inside".

A guy in his fifties with a giant beer belly, wearing dirty pants and a muscle shirt is brought in by a happy-looking cop. The gallery is on their toes. "Gotta be a super". The man is charged with dumping three garbage cans of refuse onto a parked car. The judge asks him "Why?" The man responds that he had placed a chair in the street to save the spot for his building's furniture delivery. The car owner moved the chair and took the spot. When the super told him the situation, the car owner told him "tough noogies" and left. The judge laughs and tells the super not to do it again. The gallery applauds.

A woman in her forties, looking terrified, is escorted in with a younger man, who doesn't look well. He appears tense and jumpy. The gallery whispers "junkie". The woman is charged with assault by the younger man. He is her son, who has stolen the rent money, pawned her TV and other belongings to pay his drug debt. She waited for him outside in the street, and when he returned, she pummeled him in full view of the neighborhood. When the police arrived, they saw her whacking the daylights out of him.

The gallery is mixed. One side says he is sick and needs treatment, the other says she should have hit him more often when he was younger. A smaller portion thinks she should have taken him inside. The judge tells her the "next time (after he comes back from treatment) he steals your stuff, call the police and charge him". He fines her but adds, "Payment deferred until next court appearance.

"That means don't come back here again," he says. The gallery nods their approval.

Nine women, all wearing short skirts, low-neck tops, heavy makeup and carrying small pocketbooks are brought in by five officers who are yukking it up. The gallery is stymied. "What did they do?" Everyone knows they're prostitutes, but they are mystified by what could be the charge. The women are also accompanied by a small, Asian man.

The police were called when there was a melee inside the office of a run-down, far west side hotel with hourly rates. Seems the women had been telling the Asian owner that he was to supply new sheets and towels on each rental, and he didn't. The battle had been escalating for days and the women had started to lose customers because of the condition of the beds. They banded together, and when he went to the deli on the corner for his coffee and sandwich, they raided the office and took the hotel's take for the night. They took too long divvying up the money and were caught when he returned. A fight ensued. The judge looked to the gallery. It was a beautiful moment, because "It" was a complex value decision. The women were making money "illegally" but were not being charged with prostitution. The Asian guy was obviously cheating them, but he wasn't being charged with that. They were caught counting money, but technically had not yet stolen it. The fighting was on both sides, without a witness as to who started it. One gallery male shouts, "Throw them all out!" The judge agrees.

A small, East Indian man is brought in by the arresting cop, wearing a stained, white t-shirt. Two business-like Asian men stand on the other side of the cop. The story goes that the small man stole a large amount of meats and sauces from the local Malaysian restaurant's kitchen. He was running down the street, carrying it all in a cardboard box, when he tripped and fell right on top of it. The two restaurant owners say they witnessed the event.

The gallery can't stop laughing when the man tells the judge that he didn't steal it—he "found it" and "just picked it up".

A large young man is brought forward in handcuffs by two serious-looking cops. He is subdued as he hangs his head. "Ouch!" says the gallery. They broadcast that, whatever he did, he is guilty as charged.

An elderly couple stands behind the officers. It seems the man-mountain broke down their apartment door after they did not respond to his knocking. He had intended to come to his girlfriend's apartment, and when she didn't answer the door, he, in his alcohol-fueled paranoia, became convinced she was cheating on him. Why is the old couple there? They live in apartment 2A, while the girlfriend lives in 3A.

"It's" in the Subway

To start off, you need a big subway—the bigger the better. The reason is because it must run all night, and smaller subways don't do that. So, we are talking major cities like New York, Paris, London, Madrid, and Berlin, to name a few. What can you learn about "it" on the subway?

First thing you need is some time to ride around. In New York, for example, by switching trains and taking it the full length, you can ride for over twenty-six hours without ever repeating a ride. I think that should be a college course. Your exposure to the world of people riding below will have taken you to every continent. You will probably see all the major religions of the world and hear most of its languages.

Let's start in the morning. You take your seat in downtown and watch the commuters as you head uptown. Your first impression will likely be *What a mix!* People dressed in workman clothes, while others are wearing suits and ties; women in business suits, wearing sneakers, (the work shoes are in the tote); kids with ear buds in their ears, dressed in various school regalia. The tourists are mixed in and foreign languages can be deciphered, except for the African man making clicking noises. The non-workers can be spotted by their clothing, in various shades of distress.

In any train car you will see multiple races, and the color spectrum seems to represent everyone. As Midtown passes, many of the suits have gotten off, replaced by people heading to more residential areas. Messengers with bicycles appear. Scooters and folded skateboards show up. Seems like everyone has a multiple-method journey. Moms with new-fangled, fold-up baby strollers appear. Old people can now be seen, sitting quietly with their eyes closed. Depending on the season and the weather, the same ride can have very different looks. New York is dark colors in the winter and in rain. The opposite is true in warm weather.

By the time you reach uptown, you are already a little overwhelmed by the variety of people you have seen. As the train makes its way through different neighborhoods, the riders' skin tones and languages change. Going through Harlem means more African Americans, and if you have teenagers in the car, the music will be pumping. As you swing over to the East Side and the Hispanic population boards, the music changes and people tend to dance. Pockets of school kids talk about what's "in" and what's "hot".

As you pass the upper East side, the clothing gets significantly more expensive as the train is now headed to Midtown. Tourists pack in and you hear all the different languages. There is a flurry of maps and cell phones. You hear snippets of conversations and can tell who knows where they are going and who doesn't. If the train is headed for the boroughs, you're in for ethnic diversity. If you want to "see the world", ride a train through Brooklyn. Everyone has their own neighborhood. From Hasidic Jews, to Russians, to Islanders from the Caribbean, to every Central and South American country, to all Eastern European countries, to the Asian neighborhoods of the Japanese, Korean, and Chinese (who have their own language area in Chinatown). Recently, more Southeast Asian countries like Vietnam, Cambodia, and Thailand are represented.

You have been on the train for only an hour, during the morning on a weekday. If you take the same train in the evening, you will have a completely different experience. No longer will you see suits and businesspeople. The evening ride is also different from the late-night ride, which can be a bit dicey. The underbelly of the city sleeps on the train. These days, there are more homeless people carting their belongings in plastic bags. Due to the mental health crisis, more people in need of treatment are on the streets and riding the trains. They can be dangerous, violent, depending on their conditions at any given moment.

The best experience for learning "it" is when the train has fewer passengers and you can overhear to conversations. Here's where your ethical culture course begins: listening to conversations about food from different cultures is fascinating. What people eat depends on their country of origin and what was available. Discussions over where the "best" comes from are common. Discussions about clothing as to style and taste reflect not only financial status but the overall aspect of acculturation. Mothers and daughters describe the process of hair weaving, while young black men argue over the shorter, buzz cuts versus the traditional "Afro".

Listen to Italian men argue over the best restaurants, while Cajuns assert that New Orleans has the best cuisine in the world. Brazilians argue passionately over *fútbol* (soccer), and if there are any English or Irish soccer fans on the train, a fight may break out. French tourists complain they cannot smoke in the outside cafés. Small-town American tourists in culture shock marvel at the size of New York City.

Education on the subway is limitless as well as unpredictable. On any day, the configuration of people is happenstance and that is what makes it so fascinating. Cultural variations are right in front of you. In the dead heat of summer, you can expand your horizons by observing what people wear—or don't wear—ranging from the Sunday Times fashion section to "This is all I got". On the same train there could be Muslim women, covered from head to toe in black burkas, to American teens in short shorts with skimpy tops showing their latest tattoos. Gay men wearing very short pants are in stark contrast to construction workers in jeans, boots, and helmets.

The older couples are vulnerable to the fast-moving, younger crowd when it comes to getting in and out of the trains and navigating the stairs. It's interesting to note that, in the wild, urban landscape, you can still observe moments of kindness as people help one another instead of knocking them out of the way. I saw a young, Hispanic man, taking the subway steps two at a time, stop in his tracks to assist an elderly woman who was struggling with a cart of groceries.

The ritual of giving your seat to an elderly person or pregnant woman still exists, and it crosses all ethnic groups. I saw a fifty-year-old Hispanic woman give her seat to a seventy-year-old white man, and then she proceeded to scold the self-absorbed teenagers on the train, telling them they should be the ones giving up their seats.

To hear parents teaching their children about life on the train is worth the cost of the fare. For example, a Midwest tourist mother explains to her eight-year-old why the African woman is wearing a glittering turban with massive gold hoop earrings. Another parent explains to their six-year-old why one man has no shoes.

One unique ride is the train that goes to the beach. Coney Island is the last stop at the ocean for the beach-going crowd. You can get on in Midtown, wearing your bathing suit and carrying your water tube and ice cooler, and sit next to a Ukrainian family all dressed for the wedding two stops before the ride's end. You'll probably see a bunch of teenage boys who are going to see how many hot dogs they can eat at Nathan's, or the high school girls in pursuit of that special Snapchat moment on the Ferris Wheel.

On game day, the subway is filled with fans wearing their team jerseys or caps. When the Yankees play the Mets, it's known as the Subway Series, because the subway takes you to both ball parks: the Yankees' in the Bronx and the Mets' in Queens. The ride from Manhattan can have both fans on the same train, so be prepared to hear fans talking good-natured smack. In basketball season, the Knicks from Manhattan play the Nets from Brooklyn; in hockey season it's the Manhattan-based Rangers versus the Islanders of Queens. New York City is passionate about its sports teams—don't be the only one in a crowd wearing a jersey from an opposing team.

On parade days, the subway takes on the theme of the parade, whether it's St. Patrick's Day, Thanksgiving, Gay Pride, Halloween, or Caribbean Day. The costumes and revelry are not to be missed. Just look at the books on subway photography to see how the styles have changed over the years. You can usually tell the fashion of the city by who wears what on the subway.

Musicians have found a new venue for selling their CDs and DVDs. They have to audition to play in the subway. The permit application process requires that they audition and maintain a certain level of professional behavior in order to busk. You can hear a free cello, violin, or flute concert performed by Julliard students while you wait for your train. An elderly Chinese man may be playing what looks like a cello with only one string. There are old-time jazz bands. And the new, miked-up rappers play soundtracks and improvise over them. One of the best I ever heard was a man who sang "Jackson" a la Johnny Cash with his female "June Carter" partner. There is also a BB King-inspired old bluesman who plays in the tunnel on W. 4th Street. He takes requests and I heard him do a bang-up job on "Let the Good Times Roll".

Uptown, in the bigger passageways, you can find dance ensembles that can be very good. My all-time favorite was the piano on wheels and jazz ensemble that did Dave Brubeck's "Blue Rondo A la Turk". I felt like I was back at Basin Street East.

The culture of New York in all its varied forms can be seen for the price of one ride on the subway. Be prepared to see people you may not have seen before. Be ready to listen to viewpoints from all over the globe. Hear conversations that challenge your point of view. See the human condition from top to bottom and come away from it all happy as hell that you can witness it all in one setting. Fabulous.

"It" Has Saved My Life

I don't have a belief in any organized religion as I find the concept of God beyond my ability to believe. However, there have been a few events in my life that I cannot find the answer as to why they happened. The best answers go from just plain luck, to happenstance, to "I don't have a clue". Most people in my situation would have said, "Thank God" because that is to what or whom they would have attributed their fate. Let me give you a few examples.

I was in the passenger seat with my buddy, driving home from a long road trip. We were in the left lane of the Pennsylvania Turnpike, doing about 60mph, headed east on a clear, weekday afternoon. A car driven by a young driver in the center lane cut in front of us too sharply and his left rear bumper hit our front right bumper, sending us toward the guardrail dividing east from west traffic. Reacting, my buddy turned the wheel right a little too much, and we careened across the middle lane into the right lane. This all happened in a split-second. My friend turned the wheel back to the left and, because of centrifugal force, the rear end of our car spun around and we were now going backwards, headed for the guardrail once more—except there was no guardrail in this particular section of the Turnpike.

We shot backwards, straight across the three westbound lanes of oncoming traffic. It should have been "lights out" right there—a horrific, head-on crash. Big semi-trucks, trailers, and sedans were all whizzing by at high speeds. For whatever reason, however, we sailed across three lanes unscathed and wound up in the westbound shoulder in total shock.

We were trembling in disbelief as we emerged from the car. My friend could not get his leg to stop shaking and he had to lie down. We had no idea what we had done to the car, because while it was in drive, we had just reversed the wheels at 60mph. We discovered that the engine had shut off.

We got back in the car and *voilà!* The engine started up like nothing had happened. We looked around: it was a normal day on the Pennsylvania Turnpike. No one had stopped and those who witnessed it had just kept on driving, with a story they certainly would be telling at the dinner table that night.

We had to drive to the next westbound toll booth and had to explain to the toll taker why we had an eastbound ticket. He stopped traffic and permitted us to make a U-turn and we once again headed east. We drove past the scene of the nearly fatal ac-cident and saw our tire tracks: we had crossed three lanes of traf-fic—twice—and we didn't have a scratch on us.

When I told my friend, fifty years later, that I was going to tell the Turnpike story in a book, his leg began to shake. My late mother attributed my survival to the "force" that had been protecting me all my life. She believed it was my father, who had died when I was a teen, looking out for me. Her mystical explanation had a nice feel to it.

About five years later, I was on my motorcycle, riding around Manhattan from the FDR on the east side to the west side highway. I was in the middle lane, going about 50mph, when I hit a very deep pothole around Canal Street. Usually, in this scenario, the front wheel will turn and the bike will spill. This time, however, the force of the impact sent me up in the air and all that remained connected to the bike were my hands, on the handgrips. My body was prone with my stomach on the seat and my legs flat out behind me. In other words, I had no way to put my foot on the brake or reach the handgrip breaks. If you are familiar with how the throttle works, it is in the right handgrip, and if you rotate it towards you, it increases the speed of the bike. To decrease, you have to turn it forward or away from you. Because I was just holding on I had no ability to decrease the speed.

At the same time, I was steering the bike in traffic and still going 50mph. In order to slow down, I would have to pull myself forward to gain enough slack to fully grasp the handgrip and rotate it forward. It was impossible to do because I had to steer through the curves as the West Side Highway wound its way uptown.

I really don't know how I did it, but I was approaching the 72nd Street exit after riding two miles in my handicapped state. There was a grassy area that led uphill to Riverside Drive. Though I was unable to see behind me, I steered the bike into the righthand lane and headed for the turf. I let go of the bike and fell to the right, hitting the ground hard and rolling up to the base of the slope.

When I got up, I was covered in grass stains and dirt but nothing was broken. The most amazing part was that I did not hit my head. I was not wearing a helmet—they were not required then. The bike had struck the hillside and the back wheel was still running, but it was horizontal and off the ground. No major damage. I walked it to the exit and took the city streets back down to the Village. I should not have survived that accident. I didn't even tell my mother—I just thanked my father.

My next motorcycle story was when I quit riding. I took Mikey, the manager of the White Horse, for a small spin around the block. He had been pestering me for a ride for weeks as I used to leave the bike in front of the Horse during my shifts as bartender. I did not know he had never ridden on a bike before. He got on back and I told him to hold on as we took off from Eleventh Street and headed up Hudson. The street was full of delivery trucks, cars, taxis, and assorted traffic coming out of the Holland Tunnel.

We had made it only one block when he leaned back and threw his arms into the air. You can't do that on a motorcycle without changing the weight distribution. He, being a big guy, had put too much weight backward and the front wheel came up so high that he fell off the bike. I could not control the bike as it was now coming back on me. I had to let it go as it fell to the right and I dove left.

There we were, sprawled in the center of Hudson Street: me, Mikey, and the bike. Traffic is veering to avoid hitting us as horns honked and cars are either whizzing past us or hitting their brakes. It was about one minute of chaos as drivers passed us, screaming and cursing.

We gathered ourselves, with only minor skin burns; the bike had a twisted mirror and some chrome scrapes but was fundamentally sound. We got out of the street and walked back to the Horse, with Mikey telling everyone I did not know how to ride. I decided that my motorcycle days were over after surviving two bad spills.

I was in the Bavarian Alps in Berchtesgaden, located in the southern tip of Germany, near the Austrian border. It was early December and I was there for a retreat on Jewish theology. I was trying to fill in a lot of the blanks in my heritage.

Each day would add from four to seven inches of new snow. To the locals it was normal, and they would clear the roads all the time. If you live in the Alps, you have vehicles and clothing that protect you in this environment. I have to say, as someone who is not a fan of cold, ice, or snow, it was beautiful when the sun came out as it did each day. The Alps are magnificent, and the winding roads reveal spectacular views.

Our group had just come back from the meeting room which was in a small synod next to the hotel. We decided to go by car to the café-bakery about a mile away and off the main road about a quarter of a mile. We had just turned off the main road when the radio interrupted and announced a flash avalanche had been reported about two miles above Berchtesgaden. They advised everyone to get off the roads and stay indoors. Little did we know the avalanche was to miss Berchtesgaden center but would hit everything east of it: that's where we were.

We raced the car as fast as it would go and pulled off into an area near a sawmill. We had just parked next to the south side of the mill when the avalanche hit the area from the north. It made a lot of noise and completely obscured any view. It did not last long—my guess was two minutes. It left about three feet of snow, relatively nothing in the avalanche world, but if it hits your car while driving, it just takes you with it, barreling down the mountainside. We were protected by having the mill between us and it.

Within thirty minutes, the efficient German snowplows were clearing the main road. The workers at the mill had their own plows and they were able to clear the small road so that we could exit. We were told to wait for the siren which indicated that the roads were now passable.

Had we left two minutes later from the hotel we would have had a whole different story. I connected the Jewish retreat to my father and his Austrian birthplace and assumed that this "it" was easy for him, as we were on his home turf.

On my first day of being sent to work at the stockade in Mannheim, Germany, I was on my way to bring my paper-work to the company commander's office. I worked at the Main Headquarters Hospital in Heidelberg, but this facility was a mil-itary police company that was in charge of the stockade. This company had a real military feel to it as it had tanks and armored, weapon-mounted vehicles. Platoons of soldiers were marching around.

I parked my car next to the commander's office and walked between a parked, 2.5-ton troop transport (commonly referred to as a deuce and a half) and the office's outer wall. As I got to the door, I heard a horrific noise and a simultaneous scream. A tank making a left turn had turned too sharply and hit the back of the deuce, pushing it up against the wall I had just passed. It had pinned a soldier walking behind me and crushed him to death. Just like that, it was over for that poor soldier.

I dreamt of this for years, and it makes me shake to write about it now. Ten seconds was the difference between him and me. I have heard way too many stories where one man bent over to pick up something and the bullet hit the next person in line. So much of life is played out where "it" can go one way or another, without any specific meaning, except for the people directly involved. So far, for me, I have been exceedingly lucky—or there is an "it" factor protecting me.

Spirits in the Night

In the eternal search for "it", people go on pilgrimages, retreats, weekend forays to the woods, the ocean, the desert, or the mountains, trying to obtain peace of mind and body or just plain insight. Some fast, others eat special foods, and others take herbal medicines or nothing at all. It is a seemingly endless search for meaning as to what "it" is all about. Sometimes, you don't have to go anywhere as "they" will come to you. Who, you ask? The Spirits of the Night, as I call them. They will find you in your bed, or wherever you may be. These are the voices that wake you up in the dark of night to whisper some ancient truth from your ancestors.

Ever had a mystical experience that you can't immediately categorize? Not fully awake, but not asleep, but somewhere in between when all your channels are open? People hear voices all the time. Some of them are suffering from a mental condition that medicine will eliminate. Others hear voices that they recognize, and they receive messages. Other voices are unrecognizable, but there is a message of some kind to be deciphered. Reactions vary from welcoming to being frightened.

One woman told me the story of a woman she knew who had a very stressful life and, to ease the anxiety it produced, she would sit quietly on a blanket in her backyard during the full moon and await the Spirit of the Night. It was a calming experience, and the reassuring voice she heard was a welcome gift. Was she crazy? Did she "will" it to happen? Was it something she projected? Or maybe it was the reward she sought after, like others who pray for guidance?

I had one true Spirit of the Night visitation. It could not have come at a better time. I was just sixteen and it was about three months after my father had died. I was suffering with the loss, feeling alone and crying myself to sleep each night.

I was awakened by what seemed to me to be a cloud of reddish-brown dust that had filled the space at the foot of my bed. It felt warm. I gazed at it without fear. Then, it transformed into my father and he spoke to me. He looked directly at me and said, "Don't feel bad, Kenny. I am okay, and you should be too." He smiled at me and then he vanished.

Immediately, something lifted out of me and I felt better. I was now fully awake and knew this was not a dream. I had *seen* and *heard* my father! He never visited again, no matter how hard I tried to make it happen. I would go to his grave and knew he was no longer there: only his shell was in the ground. You could say I projected what I needed, some comfort and solace to a frightened teenager. You could also say it was a spirit doing what spirits do.

But, you could also say that it was the beginning of a lifelong protective relationship between my dead father and me.

I have heard similar experiences from other people who have suffered loss or trauma. Most of those experiences they cannot explain, but know they occurred. A person told me he was hiking in the woods and came to a fork in the trail. Both paths looked equally trod upon. As he went to go right, he heard the word "No" and a gust of wind pushed him toward the other path. Not wanting to tempt fate, he took the path he was guided toward. He read in the papers a few days later that a man was found hanging from a tree in the area where he had been. He just looked at me after he told the story and offered no explanation as to who or what that was all about.

A woman I dated had many childhood traumas and she would say that, since then, she had been directed by "a voice" at significant moments in her life. She told me about some instances.

She had met a man who seemed to be fine and they had one date. When he called to ask for a second date, she heard the word "danger" while he was talking to her. It scared her so much that she quickly made her excuses and hung up the phone. She was torn between wanting to see him again or listening to an unknown voice that seemed to be a direct warning. She chose to not see him again. A few months later, she read that he had been arrested for assault and attempted rape.

I am not saying that I understand these voices or spirits in the night, or that they can be proven to exist by any known scientific method. I do know that a whole culture of indigenous people believes in the voices of their ancestors and includes them in their day-to-day lives. These ancestors are welcomed, and their voices are sought after for guidance and understanding. The Mexicans celebrate the Day of the Dead, where graves are covered with flowers and families bring food and eat at the gravesites. In the villages, tables are prepared with plates for visitors to sit with the decorated skeletons and share a meal. It is inclusive and not frightening. Mexican children are not afraid of skeletons—they decorate them with humor and respect at the same time. The cultural belief is that the dead are included in life. The concept of "Spirits in the Night" fits perfectly with the Mexican belief system and may be part of the explanation for "it".

Wanting guidance and receiving it are two very different needs. So many people seek guidance from every possible vantage point. Churches, temples, and mosques provide structure and rituals to obtain guidance. Some even provide direct, one-on-one visits with specific advice. People follow gurus, healers, and shamans in order to gain knowledge and understanding. Others sit and meditate to find an inner world of peace and tranquility. I say, whatever works is the right way. I also know that guidance can come at any time in any place. Most of mine has come from conversations with the people I have met on my journey.

When you are hungry for knowledge, it comes in many forms. My road experience showed me life in so many ways that there was no common denominator. City versus rural life, each offered something you couldn't get by choosing the other. Life in crowded cities with unlimited choices versus rural beauty and nature. Which one? I learned there was no one way to do anything, despite what my mother said. The wisdom came from people from every walk of life and philosophy. I searched for "it" everywhere—and I found it wasn't only people who were alive who were doing the teaching.

You Can Find It in Jail

One of the first things to learn is to "never go there". Sometimes it's not your fault. The judicial system has a long history of injustice as to why people go to jail. Innocent persons in the justice system are part of a sad saga: people arrested by dishonest police, convicted and sent to jail by corrupt judges or compromised juries. It has been historically a constant sore spot for all concerned, from the prisoners and their families, to the police, lawyers, judges, and civic and legislative groups all trying to make it work better. Many have been sent to jail by honest misidentifications or being represented by incompetent lawyers. Many other factors not connected to crime have sent multitudes to jail. Prejudice and poverty intertwine in the perception of who is likely to commit a crime and that starts the ball rolling. Pre-conceived notions are tough to change. Many movies and books currently reveal an inside look into police mentality, the "blue wall of silence" and resultant community distrust. There seems to be no end to television police shows that make these points.

Most people in jail have broken the law and are responsible for why they are there. Sometimes the law is the problem, as it can be outdated and non-representative of current education or community values. Some inmates are doing twenty-to-thirty-year sentences for soft drug usage, while other non-inmates are smoking weed legally, walking around free. It really hurts if you are still in jail and everyone knows you shouldn't be there. Courts are bound to enforce the law, and whether they agree or not is irrelevant. Appeals courts are very busy places.

I had the opportunity to work in two jails. One was a jail for minors and the other was a US Army stockade in Germany. The kids' jail, "juvie" as it was called, was a place for minors who had committed various offenses. Set up as a deterrent for inner city children, it was connected to the Juvenile Justice system. Kids who were on their way to a life of crime were sent to "juvie" to learn their lessons. Concept never really worked, as the kids learned how to commit crimes with more stealth and not get caught, rather than learning the concept of how bad jail can be. The error in thinking was that you can't really do bad things to kids in jail. Some of the kids had it better there than they did at home. Inner city lifestyle does not always support consistent parenting, a steady supply of food, and a nurturing environment. Jail for these kids was more stable, with a built-in prisoner community of like values, which made them immune to the "punishment". Add social workers, teachers, and community liaison workers and jail was a comfortable place to be for most of these kids. My job was to bring in the families, for I felt they needed to be prepared for their child's return. Sometimes *they* were the problem, and not the child or the "system". My goal was to coordinate support for more effective parenting. I found group family sessions offered the best forum for the sharing of ideas and experiences. The healthier families proved to be the most effective vehicle for offering alternative methods of dealing with this difficult young population. It was more about education and guidance. The kids' jail provided a forum that could not be duplicated anywhere else: when your kid is in jail, you attend the sessions.

I found that the only real edge the jail staff had was with kids sixteen or seventeen years of age, because in a year or two the same behavior would land them in the adult system—and that was a whole different ballgame. Instead of watching tv in the common room with a bunch of similar kids, they would be in county lockup with some nasty adults. Forget a dorm room environment. They were placed in a cell and they stayed there all day long. When the reality of that difference reached their adolescent minds, their faces lost color. Once a month, we would link-chain the juvie kids together and van them over to get a look at real jail. It changed some of them.

My other jail was in Germany, when I was drafted into the Army during Vietnam. Not everyone knows the Army has jail. But it is a *real* jail, with bars and electric lock gates. My office was in C-wing, which meant I had to go through seven locks to get to my office. Prison safety protocol required only one gate be open at a time. You waited for the guard to buzz you into the corridor. Then, you waited while the next guard buzzed you out.

The prison population varied greatly from homesick teenage kids who got drunk, passed out somewhere and missed roll call only to find themselves Article 15'd and sent to the stockade to await their court date, to soldiers who had committed felonies including rape and murder. My job was to do psychiatric mental status evaluations on every prisoner. I interviewed them, got their histories and documented their mental processes. The psychiatrist read my report before doing his interview. We compared notes and that was how I learned and improved. The Army requires you to be sane to stand trial, just as it is in civilian court.

The other part of my job was to do crisis intervention therapy—that was a whole lot of fun with prisoners. These guys wanted my approval because I could write a report that would be favorable to their court case. They would try every con job to convince me how they had made a mistake and learned their lesson. Most of their offenses followed a night of drinking and maybe a bar fight where someone got hurt and the MPs were called.

Minor offenses included, for example, stealing from other soldiers or getting caught with drugs. My favorite population was the "heavy" guys in D block. They were in isolated cells, one floor below the population in the basement. No windows. They all were charged with manslaughter, aggravated assault (using a weapon), or murder. They were awaiting trial and, depending on the result, were most likely being shipped back to the States to do time at Leavenworth Federal Prison in Kansas. I ran group therapy with them. Of course, we remained in D block, but I received permission to have them leave their cells to sit in chairs in a circle in the hall by the janitor's closet. There were seven men and me.

They loved it, because one, they got out of their cells, and two, they could have face-to-face conversation. The most interesting conversations I ever had were during those sessions.

Men who made one mistake on a single day now had to face the consequences of their actions. It meant their whole lives. Serious stuff. These men were not killers, although they had killed: a punch in a bar brawl knocks a guy down and he hits his head on a radiator pipe and dies; a scuffle on a train platform results in someone falling onto the tracks; a guy catches his girlfriend cheating and pushes the naked lover out the door—he falls down the steps and breaks his neck. I heard stories like those all the time.

The most difficult experience for me was visiting American Army prisoners who were sent to German jail. Those men had committed crimes on German soil and were tried in German courts. Germany had the option to exercise its right to try these men rather than letting it fall to the US Army. German jail is rough: it is five levels below ground. The farther down you are, the more serious your crime. The elevator went only to the next floor below. You exited and walked a long corridor and took a new one to the next level. This arrangement made escape impossible.

NATO rules dictated that any American military prisoner sent to German jail must be visited monthly, by Army personnel, to report on their health and mental status. I visited these men in their sunless environment. The authority of German jail contrasted significantly with American. The rules of conduct were clear: "You do what you are told to do—you didn't listen on the outside, but you will learn to listen here." The difference was the prisoners were not demeaned. They were not bullied or treated harshly. German jail philosophy involved rehabilitation and skill-learning, so when and if they got out, they were less likely to return. German thinking was that, once they had paid their debt, they should go and be productive. This contrasted to the American system where their crimes followed them into their futures and restricted their ability to work or function as free citizens, or even have the right to vote.

In Germany, the prison staff was not your enemy, but they enforced appropriate sanctions if someone chose to not comply. Very few incidents of refusal were reported. The more they complied, the easier their jail experience. Good behavior was rewarded with more freedom and benefits.

Most of the soldiers were resigned to their lives in prison and formed their own support communities among other inmates. They learned the language and left most of their American soldier mentality or identity behind. It was chilling to witness. Only the violent offenders, while in jail, had a cell. Everyone else lived in a dormitory environment. The saddest comments were about their dreams of sunshine.

There were the other crimes committed by soldiers serving in Vietnam. That was a whole other ball of wax. They involved drug abuse, mental illness, alcoholism or just plain desperation. Some of these men intentionally shot themselves just to get out of Vietnam. Some went crazy in battle and the Army sent them to Wiesbaden Air Force Base. My prison got the overflow. Bases in Hawaii and Japan were heavily covered by the media, but Germany was not on the media map. It was a way for the Army to limit visibility as to what was really happening. Vietnam War mental illnesses were mainly the paranoid variety. The soldiers didn't know who to trust because, for example, the little Vietnamese lady who cleaned the barracks for a few months could leave a bomb on her next visit.

You never really saw the enemy, but you heard them. There were tunnels under all the Army bases and Viet Cong snipers would pop up like moles, kill, and then disappear back into the tunnels. It drove the soldiers crazy.

I kept a log of every prisoner interview. Most of the crimes committed by soldiers stationed in Germany were of the minor variety, which meant after time served, they were returned to active duty. Time served in jail did not count against their tours of duty. If they had sixteen months to do before they went to jail, they had sixteen months to do when they were released.

There is something about the Uniform Code of Military Justice (UCMJ) I need to explain. In the military, an officer is considered an officer of the court. If he or she declares an enlisted man did something wrong, then he did something wrong. So, when that enlisted man got his day in court, it was run by officers, as no enlisted man can be a judge or sit on the panel. So much for a jury of your peers. Military trials have no juries, just a panel of officers. Rank is what counts in the military. If you are a young officer on a military panel, you don't disagree with your superiors—not if you want to get promoted. To me, it felt like my guy had no chance in court whatsoever. It was like a poor black man in the South being in court with an all-white judge and jury. Boy, we needed Spencer Tracy or Atticus Finch. No enlisted man ever outranked the lowest ranking officer. A first-year lieutenant outranked a twenty-two-year sergeant major. That was just the way it was.

The courts began on the premise that a soldier was guilty because an officer had accused him, and by statute they were imbued with honesty—so much for innocent until proven guilty. The UCMJ required that you prove your innocence. I saw this mind-boggling process firsthand as I went to court with these soldiers. There is a sad and bitter adage that states: "Military justice is to justice as military music is to music."

Having learned how the system worked and how all the players functioned in this steamroller environment, "it" helped me see victims where I had never seen them before. The insider prison belief was that the innocent people were the prisoners, and the criminals were running the place. To be fair, that was true in only some jails, but enough to rock your view of the court and prison system. I will leave the discussion of "for profit privatized jails" for another day. Who could possible think that there might be incentives to putting people in jail?

"It" Only Looks That Way

I will give you an example of a family who came to see me: this one is a composite, derived from many families with similar issues. A well-known family of excellent community standing came to see me in my office. They spent an inordinate amount of time going over confidentiality rules and all their possible ramifications. First signal: it wasn't going to be pretty. Who speaks first in family sessions is always significant.

Dad took the floor and said that there was a thief in the house. Everyone hung their heads—except the eleven-year-old girl, Enid, who looked straight at me and nodded in assent. This was a rather large family: Mom, Dad, and six kids ranging in ages from five to eighteen. Mom's eyes got wide when Dad said he had to work a lot of hours.

Ok, we had a mystery. Welcome to lesson one of family dynamics: someone, or maybe more than one, isn't telling the truth. To maintain family harmony and balance, I asked Dad to tell me about his family, but nothing about the thievery. There was a bevy of success stories, awards, trophies, scholarships and community service. My first image was the cover of the Saturday Evening Post with this Rockwell family sitting in Adirondack chairs on the porch.

Mom spoke next, saying that she was proud of her children and that they were hard-working, loving, kind, and generous. She added that she was flabbergasted by the current situation, and frankly embarrassed to even be in the room. "It", she felt, should have been solved at home. The oldest male child, Robert, spoke up and said that Dad had tried, but it had only led to screaming and finger-pointing.

The first intervention was to acknowledge that not everyone was there by choice and how conflicting that can be. I noted that sometimes when there was a plumbing problem and Dad couldn't fix it, you needed to call in the expert. Everyone can be affected by the problem, and sometimes it feels good to not have to be the one to fix it.

I told the family that I would be counting on their input in order to help me solve the problem with them. I would first meet with them individually, in order to get to know them more personally. I asked if that was ok with everyone. I looked at them individually to assess their attitude about consent. Only Robert gave a reluctant nod.

So what problem were we solving? The conversation became lively with all but the five-year-old boy participating. There had been a string of things gone missing. From money to jewelry, from homework to the latest being Enid's highly secret diary—which was found in her sister Maura's desk by Mom. Maura vehemently denied stealing it. Dad was quite angry about people not respecting boundaries, and that his money clip was discovered in Enid's backpack. She was defended by all as least likely to steal it. She kept shaking her head no. I told them that I would use the next sessions to meet with them all individually.

Ok. Shenanigans were going on. Finding the truth is best left to detectives, but therapists have their own slant on the hidden reasons why people do things and why they lie about it. We are trained to look for alliances and allegiances in families. They emerge when conflict surfaces, and this family was under stress with their first real encounter with acting out. The three middle children, all female, were eight, eleven, and thirteen. It would be a handful for any family to have three children of middle school age, the toughest time in anyone's developmental process. The two oldest boys were Robert and Thomas, respectively.

When they returned, I spoke to Dad first. He was forty-eight, a local lawyer and church elder, and a community fund-raiser. He had five siblings. Mom, age forty-six, was in advertising before she became a full-time mother. She was a "chin-up" kind of person who did everything and bore it well. I sensed some conflict with the husband, which was common in large families where the father worked long hours and everything on the domestic front fell to the mother.

Youngest boy, Steven, was five and an energetic, happy boy. He wished his brothers weren't so old and that they could play with him more. He spent a lot of time with the nanny. Eight-year-old Sara was quiet and reserved—unusual in a family, as the younger kids tend to get louder earlier as they learn the tricks from the older siblings. Enid, eleven, was not as athletic as her older sister and wished she could be. She was Mom's helper in all ways and was perceived as being a bit sad and struggling with early adolescence. Maura, thirteen, was all things successful: athletic, a good student, popular. She proudly proclaimed that she was Dad's favorite—but "don't tell". Thomas, fifteen, had been a great student but struggled now. He was upset that he was the last cut from the high school basketball team that his brother was on. He thought his sisters yelled about nothing. Robert, eighteen, was a good student athlete that would be graduating soon. He had a girlfriend and didn't spend much time at home.

Got a guess as to who was doing the stealing? Let's go down the list: Not Steven: five, too young—he would easily get caught. Sara was a possibility due to her quietness, and Enid thought it was her. Enid had been cleared by everyone and was a victim of the stolen diary, but there was the money clip found in her backpack. Maura was at a prime age for this kind of behavior, but she was happy and successful and seemingly without motive. Thomas had had recent difficulties in school and had just suffered a major disappointment in being cut from the team. Possible. Robert was ruled out as he was spending so much time away from the family and thinking ahead to college.

When I asked the parents whom they suspected, Dad said he had no clue. He couldn't see any one of his kids doing that. Mom said both Sara and Thomas were having difficulties, though she doubted they could do it.

Further family sessions revealed the hidden dynamics. Sara saw Maura as the star and Mom's favorite. She said that Mom used Enid as her aide or workhorse. Sara felt left out, although Dad spent time with her and they "talked". I asked if the nanny could come to the next session, as she was part of the family. Dad objected. Mom overruled him, saying she could add some valuable information as she knew the family.

The nanny was the key as she witnessed the kids without the parents being around. When I spoke to her, she explained that Enid was jealous of her older sister, Maura, who gobbled up Mom's time and was better at everything—but Enid didn't do anything wrong, ever. Dad spent his time with Steven, and Thomas wanted to be like his brother and was the most emotional and angry about his recent failures. Robert was "already out of the house".

Got a guess now? Sara felt left out, but she had Dad. Enid was jealous and that is always a motive for sabotage, but she was a victim. Thomas was struggling, but getting involved with his sister's dynamics just didn't feel right to me. I met with Mom and Dad and told them my idea. I told them that acting out was putting into behavior what you can't put into words. Most likely, Sara was the culprit due to her quietness, but her "Get-Out-of-Jail-Free" card was that she was close to Dad and it was his money that was taken. Thomas was suspect but ruled out because of his lack of a motive of revenge on his sisters' items. He said Dad called him on the phone all the time and had been helpful.

I brought Enid into the office alone and told her I understood why she did it. Her face turned white. I told her it was hard to have an older sister who does less chores and gets more attention. It was also hard to compete with her, because she was older and involved with herself. I told her that I guessed she was angry at Dad for not seeing her problem and helping, but he was not there enough, anyway. I also said it was hard to live with yourself when everyone thinks you are so good and you know you are doing all these things. Her body said, "You are right", but her last defense was to say, "But my diary was stolen". I told her that was brilliant—putting her own diary in your sister's desk cleared you of any suspicion. With that, she cried. I told her growing up was hard, but she could find a way to use her words and tell her parents how she felt. "It's the only way," I told her. Her parents could address what she was feeling after she went through a rough patch. It would be different as I would be seeing her parents and helping them to adjust. We practiced what she might say, and I reassured her that I would be there to help her.

Dad was floored and Mom felt badly after some initial defensiveness. I told them to check in with the nanny on her view of what was going on. The family followed through and reported the stealing had stopped.

A few months later, Enid saw me in the hallway of her school one day when I was on my way to the Guidance Office. She gave me a warm smile and said, "It's better now." *It's* better now …

Kids Know "It"

Over the years, I learned to talk to kids to find out what was going on in family problems, especially younger ones who don't have sophisticated defenses or knowledge of social dynamics. Kids know when parents don't mean what they say just by their tone, as they automatically tune out the words. How many parents don't understand that kids know much more than they give them credit for? The answer is: most of them.

Kids listen from the other room when a parent talks on the phone. They creep downstairs to hear conversations when they are supposed to be upstairs sleeping. Apartment-dwelling kids hear everything, as privacy depends on wall thickness. One seven-year-old told me he puts a glass to the wall to hear what they are saying on the other side. He "saw it done on TV".

If you ever have the opportunity, watch how dogs and kids react to a family, non-physical fight. They react the same, meaning they know when it's serious and when it's not. So many times, I would get permission to talk to kids without their parents in the room. They don't really know what they are telling me, but you know it rings true. For example, "Mommy talks in a low voice to someone who calls in the afternoon"; "Mommy hides bottles and tells Daddy she never saw them"; "Mommy puts money in her underwear drawer and tells Daddy she doesn't have any"; "Daddy smokes cigarettes in the garage when he says he's quit smoking them"; "My sister talks to a boy on the computer when she tells Daddy she is doing homework."

Kids use the same truth-smelling ability with teachers, coaches, babysitters, and the general public. "Mom, that woman doesn't like you, does she?" "Why do you say that?" "Her smile was funny." Now, that is inborn body language reading. When words don't match tone or feel, kids know "it". They know when adults are uncomfortable or nervous with them as they know when the words don't match the expression. They tell me, "Oh he was just saying that." Meaning, it's not true.

The best examples are when kids try to figure out what's going on in the bedroom. "Mommy and Daddy fight and they go into the bedroom to get away from us. Then it will get quiet. Then they make strange-sounding noises. When Daddy comes out, he's usually feeling much happier. They do something in there that makes them look different."

Similarly, "Mommy doesn't tell me the truth when she wants me to feel better." "I hate it when Daddy says, 'We'll see'. It means 'no'."

These are just a few of the truths that kids deal with every day. When they get the chance, they ask really good questions. An eight-year-old asked me why his parents have friends they don't like. I asked for an explanation. He said his father had to be "talked to" by his mom for him to go out for dinner with their friends. Why is that? "Well, son …"

One kid told me his father was not very bright. "Why?" I asked. "He believes Santa Clause can bring all the kids on this block their presents with one sled." "Why is that tough to believe?" "The whole block is big apartment buildings—even UPS needs a big truck!" *Oh!*

"When Mommy wants something from Daddy, she uses her other voice." "My father always brings flowers on the night that he goes out." One little girl told me she doesn't ever want to get married. "Why is that?" "Because my mother told her friend on the phone that it makes her very sad, and she is very unhappy."

One nine-year-old-girl told me she is smarter than both of her parents. "Why do you say that?" "Because on my weekend with each one, I get whatever I want by saying I am not happy here." "Isn't that dishonest?" "No, it's true. If I don't get what I want, I will be very unhappy." Hmmm. Parenting needed. But they probably don't talk to one another and compare notes anymore. How to make a brat, lesson one.

There always comes that day when the adult in the room, who sometimes is the parent, has to tell the child about how things work in the real world, which translates as to what it's like outside the home. That's where you are no longer given things just because you are a kid. Now, you have to earn it. Kids generally parry this by slowing down the growing up process, which puts parents in a real dilemma. Too much reality makes the impending adult world an undesired experience. Too little reality doesn't prepare for eventual entry. You see it played out with teenagers who are in the wonderful world of choice: adult when they want to be, and child when they need to be. Parents always asked for guidance when the saw this duality with their children. "How can he be so responsible one day and an absolute baby the next?" "Here's how," I answer. "Close your eyes and picture a piece of Swiss cheese on a cutting board in front of you. Now, keeping your eyes closed, take an imaginary pin and stab the cheese. Sometimes you get the cheese and sometimes you get the hole. That's adolescence. Eventually, hopefully, the holes fill in."

I always parried kids' criticism of their parents with illustrations of when parents teach fearful kids a new task. The kid always says, "I can't do that." With proper encouragement and safety, the parent earns more trust and teaches the child how to swim or ride that bike, maybe even finish that impossible math problem. I would ask the child, "How did they know you could do it, when you didn't?" I was usually met with a frown before I went on: "Because parents have overcome fear, and they remember when they were in the same position as you are today. Even though they make mistakes at times, be thankful you have them, because you do need their guidance."

"My mother is too busy for me." "Daddy always looks like he wants to nap and tells me 'maybe later'." Tough positions for all involved. The over-scheduled parent is on the merry-go-round of responsibilities and is forced to constantly juggle priorities. Mistakes made in this process, by not explaining, can cause unnecessary feelings of rejection. Parents who scream at kids and call them "selfish" in these instances are reacting without an awareness of the consequences of their actions. They might try saying, "I want to play with you now, but I have to finish these chores first, and if you want to help me, I will be done sooner." The children would respond without hurt to that message.

How many kids have you seen drag out the recovery time from a minor scrape because the "attention" feels good? It feels good to adults as well. "Noticing", a form of validation, is what kids clamor for. How many times a day at the pool do we hear the phrase, "Watch me!" The adult female version is more subtle, as it's more about noticing her clothes, hair, nails, weight loss, etc. Not receiving it feels the same as it does to the child. "I am not important to him." When adults feel taken for granted, they tend to stop giving. Kids who are ignored will do the same.

Kids who learn "it" do better than those who don't. Figuring out your parent helps you with your timing and approach when you are armed with an "I want something." Little girls learn quickly how to "turn it on with Daddy to coax out a 'yes'." They learn to do what works and drop what doesn't. Boys don't do as well in this area, as they don't handle "no" well. They tend to anger quickly and quit trying, as compared to the more patient, "try another way" female response. Their fathers make the same mistakes with their mothers. They give up too quickly and don't learn how to hang in there for the final round. Girls don't give up easily, as they watch their mothers in action all day long.

The timing part is more instinctual. A good reader of body language can quickly assess mood and probability in one glance. A little girl will stop, pause, and turn around without saying anything, because they are excellent non-verbal readers. A little boy in the same situation will start speaking before he even looks. Once he sees and interprets whatever he is looking at, he will turn around and walk off in a huff. Boys do eventually learn to body-read, and when they do, a girlfriend is usually involved. How many parents have you heard say, "I said that to him all the time, and he ignored me. Now his girlfriend tells him the same thing and he listens." There is something about reward going on in this case. He will have trouble initially with the girlfriend also, but she will give him the signals. Quiet is not good. Loud is better. Beware the silent stare. *Stop asking—just keep doing what you are doing.*

Some words about praise: I earned my stripes with parents over this issue. We all know that someone's kid is the most unique individual ever born on this planet—except when they have five of them. Some parents tend to over-praise younger children in order to motivate them. It is counter-productive. If something is enjoyable, kids will want to repeat it.

Let me explain: If I do something well, I like the resulting feeling of satisfaction and I will repeat it on my own without any external reward. If I am over-recognized for my performance, this complicates the process. Before, I did it on my own because it felt good; now, I'm over-praised and I must split the reward. Did I do it for me, or for the applause?

What if I don't do it as well the next time and I get the same exaggerated reward? I have now learned that's it's not the quality of what I produce, as the parent rewards what I know to be of lesser quality. It cheapens the praise. Undeserved praise risks the value of true, earned praise later. All kids know when they don't try hard enough. Tell them that, and it reinforces their self-perception. You can learn more from failure at a young age than you can from success. Isn't that the universal lesson of trial and error?

How many times does a child say, "You are just saying that

because you are my parent and you have to say that"? How many parents respond honestly with, "You are right"? Very few. If they did, the child would be rewarded for their perceptibility and the parent can add, "I still stand behind what I said". The message is heard.

Finding "it" as a child can be quite complicated and overwhelming, especially if a parent or parents are damaged in one or multiple ways. The child is forced to navigate around bad parental advice, or a lack of it, and somehow replace it with advice that fits their world. The advice varies depending on environment: a suburban, car-pooled kid must consider different factors than a street kid from an urban metropolis. They live in opposite spectrums. Kids in the big city learn faster to overcome their fears and use their own perceptibility to foster independent judgement. Being aware, reading, and reacting are everyday behaviors. Just think of the multiple skill sets a city kid must learn by taking the subway to school on their own, rather than just hopping into the suburban van or relying on crossing guards. Talk about infantilizers! Crossing guards treat kids like they are three years old no matter how old they are. I'll save that chapter for another day. If kids dealt with the cars with some supervision, they would learn quickly how to cross the street by themselves—which is the goal, anyway.

Learning to deal with the healthy and non-healthy public is step one for learning "it". Awareness and reaction can be crucial to inner city survival. Imagine dropping off a suburban nine-year-old at the subway stop and saying, "I'll see you at five—have a good day." That is a regular day to city kids who know how to use their transportation cards, switch subway lines, navigate past a multi-cultural train ride, and avoid the various, less-than-healthy people on every street before returning home safely every day.

A suburban family day in the city results in the child or children telling me that the kids they saw were the same age as they, but they acted "way older". There is a more challenging, delicate balance for city parents who must teach both safety and independence. I always found it fascinating the way city parents explained New York street life to their children: when to "look away" and the quick summarizations were the best. "Maybe he'll find a pair of pants"; "No, he didn't have a cell phone—he's just talking"; "She will probably not sleep there when it gets cold"; "It's impolite to stare—just move on"; "The man behind the card-mover is called a 'shill'. He pretends to be a person in the audience, but he really works with the card man. It's dishonest"; "Make sure you don't touch the toilet handle with your bare fingers"; "Never go with anyone you don't know to see something special". All these lessons help the city kids find "it".

Kids have wisdom beyond their words. They know tone, inflection, and read body language well. They listen when the parents talk to each other, out of earshot. They talk to other kids and compare notes without shame or doubt. Their older siblings pass down the code of learning how to deal with Mom and Dad. There is just something so simple about childhood logic that trumps parental explanation. Depending on the child's age, kids want their world to make sense, and therefore they eliminate confusing and contradictory information and stay with their basic truth of what make sense to them, not what makes sense to adults. It's like their taste buds: they are not ready for complex combinations of spices and herbs. They enjoy simple flavor and no amount of parental explanation will make asparagus taste good. Nor will they swallow explanations of why Daddy was mean and that he did not mean to hurt their feelings. Their reality is he did, and he's going to be watched a little more carefully now. Children do not need to be told something is funny or something is scary. Remember Art Linkletter and his show *Kids Say the Darndest Things*? What they really told him was the truth from their point of view. Like I told the parents who came for parenting advice: "Listen to your children more and talk less. They will connect to you if you let them." Your parental job is to foster your kids "it" development. Just realize that their starting point is farther along than you think it is.

Detectives, Trauma, and "It"

Did you ever talk to a big city street detective? Or maybe you have one in your family? Anyway, they are a special breed. One thing for sure is they have seen more than their share. Like ENTs and ER workers, they see life at its raw edges. Trouble is, they see it daily and it's hard not to be warped by it. I have treated quite a few over the years and let me tell you, I feel for them.

One of the first issues they deal with is what do you do with all the trauma you have witnessed? Do you sit down and let yourself cry? Never. Do you go home and talk to your wife and family about it? Rarely, as the thinking about it is, "I want to get away from all that once I leave the job." Do you talk to your peers? Yes, but unfortunately it is done over drinks at the local "cop bar".

Alcohol can become a problem as it temporarily covers the trauma, but as a way of coping it has a serious downside. Most enlightened departments now provide counseling for police officers and detectives. But, as with most male-dominated cultures, getting help is seen as a sign of weakness and no one wants to be seen that way. Things are slowly changing and making counseling mandatory has taken away some of the stigma, but it is not really in their culture to think that they can't handle it. A detective told me, "It's part of the job: you see a lot of death and ugliness, and you have to deal with it."

"How?"

"By putting it out of your mind."

"Ok, but what about the dreams?"

"Oh … them. They can be a bit weird, and I have woken up screaming quite a few times."

"This tells you what?"

"Take Ambien."

And so it goes.

People on the front line of trauma all share the same experience; it stays with them far longer than they want it to. There are coping methods, such as humor. It seems brutally cold to outsiders to hear them joke about what they just witnessed, but you have to walk in their shoes to understand their gallows humor.

When I was working in the ER, they brought in a dead five-year-old child who had been run over by a car. The police photographer of thirty years was there to take photographs of the body, as per protocol. When he came out of the room, he spoke to me. "Look at this," he said, pointing to his camera. "I have been doing this for thirty years and you never get used to seeing a dead child. I just took a whole series of shots, but I never loaded the camera." He then put film in the camera and returned to the room where the deceased child lay. When he came out, he had the "blank stare" that so many trauma victims have. "I guess I am still not used to 'it'," he said.

One of my jobs was to work with the police in re-educating them about dealing with psychiatric patients and their emergencies. The police "mentality" about mental patients was not particularly sensitive: they had a low tolerance and tended to treat them as defiant or unreachable. I was there to provide alternative approaches that would not escalate to violence. The cops wanted nothing to do with this approach, as they viewed mental illness as not part of their realm. I considered it a success when they stood back and said, "I got one of yours in there—be my guest." At least the patient was not going to get beaten up.

The detectives who dealt with mental illness were more professional, as they recognized the humanity involved. One detective summed up a common view, "They don't have a clue about what 'it' is all about, and I leave that up to you people or the courts. I just don't want to get myself hurt, which is a very real possibility." I concurred.

It is difficult enough to deal with homicides and violence daily without becoming skewed about the human condition. If you are a garbage man, it's hard to not think of people as dirty and smelly, because you are picking up their refuse all day long. You may miss the flowers and the trees if you are focused on the gutter. Same goes for the detectives who do not spend enough time in reparative events. I tell them to go into open spaces and listen to music. Watch a squirrel do his routine. Listen for the birds chirping. Pet a dog. See a comedy show. Go fishing, swimming, or bike riding in the park. Go to your favorite restaurant and eat your favorite food. All these are normal, everyday things because most of their days are not ordinary.

Some cope better than others, especially if they have been able to maintain normal, family relationships. Those who are divorced or live alone do worse with coping, because "it" is very powerful and can invade their thinking with negative and destructive thoughts. Being alone intensifies the resultant feelings. Too many detectives have told me, "Listen, if it gets too bad, I can always eat a bullet," followed by, "Just joking, Doc, ya know?"

"Yeah, I know. You want to join the 'We don't eat bullets' group?"

"You have such a thing?"

"Well, you would be the first to join. Please pass the word that we want our detectives alive and well."

"Not to worry, Doc. We are all soldiers …"

"A good visual for dealing with what you do every day. Many people see "it" and learn not to let it warp them, but too many have been beaten down by "it"."

After 9/11, I was volunteering at the WTC site and my job was to talk with the men coming off the pile who had spent their day searching for the remote possibility of finding survivors instead of bodies. My message was simple: "Six months from now, or maybe a year, when you are not talking to anyone and can't sleep and are probably drinking or drugging more than you should or relying on sleep medication, you need to know it's because of what you are seeing here today. That will be the time for you to recognize what I am telling you now and to come in for post-trauma help. No one

can see this level of destruction and process it without group help."
The best response I got from the men was "Ok". The publicity
about the PTSD men and women developed following 9/11 was
widely available, but unfortunately their overall physical health was
more severely damaged due to the chemicals they ingested. Some
are still suffering. Sadly, "it" is still there.

The Animals Definitely Have "It"

We all know the animals have "it". They sense events before the happen. When I was in Hawaii, a local man told me how the Islanders know when a tsunami is coming before it's announced. The animals head for high ground, off to the volcanos.

Ever notice the noise that birds make before a storm? Dogs and cats will become agitated or hide. If you are lucky enough to live on a farm, you have everything right in front of you. The geese start honking when the air pressure changes. The chickens will gather in one spot—usually in a corner of the coop—to let you know it's soon going to thunder.

The most fascinating place to observe animals is the forest. How do they know, ahead of all man's instruments, what is going to happen? Their sensors are sharper than ours. Elephants can smell other elephants two miles away. Chimps use their large noses to smell danger from predators. A turtle will not move, based on the vibrations in the earth, if it senses danger. An eagle can see a mouse from a thousand feet in the air.

Out on the plains, the giraffes and gazelles prick up their ears when they smell a predator. In the ocean, a whale can hear for miles and they signal one another from distances far beyond what was once believed. Horses in the wild will take off before they see anything dangerous.

Wouldn't it be magical if we humans had all these extra advantages and we could prevent bad things from happening? Just think if we had a built-in bad relationship detector! Or if we could tell who isn't telling the truth by using some physiological bullshit detector? Maybe we might use our eyes like the owl and see everything more clearly. Or use the bat's sonar to avoid crashing into things. What if we could smell like the elephant does and not eat anything that was bad for us? That would be a real supermarket skill: go up and down the aisles and eliminate anything with harmful chemicals. Lots of chicken, pork, and beef would stay on the shelves and things in cans would never make it out of the store.

What if you had the rhino's mate-detector large nose? One whiff and you know this partner is not for you. Or, if you had the dog's nose in a bar and could sniff who is ready and who is not? Would save you a lot of time and drinks. I love how parrots watch the possible suitor male do his fawning, mating dance in the tree and know immediately whether he's good enough or not. It's "America's Got Talent", Macaw-style. "Sorry, Peter. You have to work on your move—what you just showed me isn't going to ruffle my feathers."

We humans should have a simple mating ritual, like the penguins. The male digs a hole for the egg and shows it to the female for her to decide whether he'll be a good provider. He also must present her with a smooth rock, which will be the foundation of the nest. No chintzy fugazi here!

The best human example is in Ugurp, in Cappadocia, Turkey, where the entire village is comprised of potters and a prospective husband has to make a perfect pot—and a perfect lid made separately, without any refitting—to show the father whether his skill is good enough to provide a suitable living for the daughter. Bad potters stay single, as the competition is fierce. This could be our version: "Okay, folks! It's marriage tryout night at the Barkley Center! Shoot ten baskets without missing, dribble blindfolded through the cones, bake a pie, and change a diaper! Come one, come all! See if you have "it"!

The Army Knows "It" Well

You have to hand it to the military, especially the Army and the Marines: they really know about "it". They can turn a lethargic, passive, frightened kid into a fighting machine in eight weeks. They can mold a juvenile delinquent a college kid, or a regular working stiff into what they want with the same approach.

It starts the minute you arrive for basic training. It doesn't matter if you joined or if you were drafted. The heavy-duty, tried and true approach is practiced universally at every base the government operates. The concept is to break you down from the way of civilian life and indoctrinate you into the military mind. Their methods can utilize every form of psychological pressure as they control your sleep, your food, and what you do every minute for eight weeks. You make no independent decisions as everything is closely choreographed by the training staff.

The first task is to take away your individuality. So, you no longer are called by your name. You are a "trainee", and everyone in your barracks is a "trainee". Your hair is shaved off like everyone else's. Uniformity is the goal as you are told you will be a soldier and if you want to survive in combat you will learn everything they teach you. They have a point. Your former life is irrelevant, and your only task is to learn how to survive in a combat zone. Forget the idea that you don't believe in war or you didn't even sign up—the reality is that you are there and the faster you adapt, the better your chances of survival.

The sound of the metal spoon crashing inside the metal garbage can is your alarm clock at 3:45 am, with the sergeant turning on the lights and screaming, "Drop your cocks and put on your socks! It's Army time!" You wake up completely jumbled and have ten minutes to use the bathroom, get dressed, and stand by your bed for inspection. The military mind of your drill instructor is like a machine. He has done this with so many platoons that you know he doesn't even see you or care. He may open his A.M. greeting with, "You know what happens when they ship your body back to the states?" He pauses, then replies, "They draft another trainee to replace you."

The mindset is all about authority and rank. Having more stripes on your arms is the goal. You, now, they tell you, are the lowest of the low, which means you must listen and obey anyone with more seniority and stripes. In the military you do not question an order, because the one giving the order has more knowledge and experience than you. In a combat zone, not following an order can cost you your life. End of story. The reality could be that he is a twenty-one-year-old psychopath with more stripes on his arm, but he is in charge of you. Well, it's not really you—it's your rank. You are taught to achieve and gain more rank.

Basic training is a slow process of learning obedience while simultaneously learning survival skills. The Army is a master of turning your soft, civilian body into a hard-as-rock muscular machine capable of doing what you never imagined it could do. The initial average weight loss is over twenty pounds as the fat melts away with running, push-ups, chin-ups, hand-to-hand combat, etc. while carrying everything on your back. Then, they build you up by increasing the mileage and the number of hours spent exercising. Running the obstacle course is a daily war zone activity. It includes climbing rope up a twenty-foot wall, swinging over water, crawling under barbed wire, finding your way through smoke, and mucking your way through mud. Then you run the four miles back to the mess hall for lunch.

Most people have never eaten as much as they do in basic training. It's three, well-balanced, full meals. You can eat as much as you want, but you can't leave anything on your plate. If you took it, you eat it. The mentality here is that you took someone else's portion and did not eat it, thereby depriving your comrade of his food. "And he could be the one who saves your life." They build a camaraderie based on an inter-dependency for survival. You want your platoon mate to be in great shape and have all the necessary survival skills because he may be the one to carry you out if you are shot.

They condition your mind by using one very powerful and effective tool. If you fall asleep in class or don't do your night watchman job perfectly, if you drop a piece of necessary equipment or if you make noise during silent time, the Army doesn't punish *you*—they punish your squad. So, the offender has to sit and watch the squad do your extra push-ups. It works beautifully. The message is simple: you are one, well-integrated fighting machine and all parts must work in sync; there are no individual parts.

About half-way through basic training, there is a change in attitude among the trainees. Civilian life seems far in the past and the present day is all that matters. Instead of groaning about every new task that is presented, whether it be grenade-throwing or ammunition-carrying, the idea is to do it better than your squad member. The men start competing to see who runs the longest, carries the most weight, or climbs highest. There is the bonus of a two-day pass for the winner of the sharpshooter contest. The one who does the most push-ups only gets a one-night pass, as being an accurate sniper rates higher on the squad scale.

Men display their original clothing as they can no longer wear the size they were issued. By the sixth week, everyone knows one another by their nickname, which was appropriately earned by universal consent. Everyone knows why a recruit is called "Horndog". Formation for mail call is fun as the sergeant calls out the nicknames earned. There are too many large last names, so "Alphabet C-z" or "W alphabet witz" are common.

Slowly but surely, the Army teaches you how to disassemble your rifle and reassemble it while blindfolded and being sprayed with a hose. You learn to care for your gas mask, rifle, and knife. You make sure your feet are dry and cared for as you are useless if you cannot move. Your head is covered in cold and wet weather because that is where you experience the most heat loss. The military knows how to keep you alive as you care for your emergency kit as if your life depended on it, which it literally does. They tell you, "We can teach you how to stay alive, but the final responsibility is yours, as there are no second chances to stay alive."

The methods used by the military can be brutal. They shame, abuse, ridicule, and demean. The use physical punishment to re-inforce what they want. They won't beat you up themselves, but it's not hard to set up a mismatch in one-on-one physical combat exercises. Two nights in a row on guard duty will teach you any lesson they want you to learn.

By the time the trainees complete basic training, they are re-ferred to as privates. Not a whole lot of military respect goes with that rank, but at least you are no longer a trainee. Plus, you get to use your last name. Remember Goldie Hawn in *Private Benjamin*? She joined the army with the condos, not the one with the bar-racks. Even she learned.

The military knows a lot about "it", referring to the making of a soldier for the inhuman condition of war. They know how the mind works. BF Skinner would be proud that his theories are proven every eight weeks. "Give me a man and let me control every aspect of his environment and I will turn him into what I want." That's "it" in a nutshell.

The Cinema

Cinema: the magical world of going someplace you have never been without having to leave your chair. The topic is huge, and by no means are we going to cover it in its entirety. The "it" in movies is what the director/screenwriter wants you to see. Maybe it's a moral, an ethic, or an attitude which demonstrates something along the continuum of right or wrong. Maybe it's just a depiction of life as it is, as the French New Wave did with its *cinéma vérité*. The camera documents and the audience absorbs, with no attempt to make you think one way or another. Or maybe it's the art of escape, an experience which lets you leave your own personal life and vault into the world of fantasy, where both bicycles and elephants can fly.

The world of cinema has changed drastically since the age of the digital camera. Films can be made now by average citizens, as film processing becomes unnecessary and costs are reduced.

Companies like Netflix, Amazon, and Hulu stream films to your phone, tablet, or computer. Some say that in ten years there will be no more movie houses as they will price themselves out of business.

So, what is "it" in a movie? Generally speaking, the "it" is what you are searching for: the "message" of the movie, its point of view and the outcome of all that you are shown, all wrapping up in one powerful conclusion.

The most common themes in movies are romance and crime, with adventure and drama not far behind. Who hasn't placed themselves inside a character on the screen? How many guys saw themselves as one of the heroes in war films? Or saw themselves as Marlon Brando or Paul Newman when they rebelled against the status quo and won the girl? How many women saw themselves as Katherine Hepburn or Meryl Streep when they stood up against men's rules? The cinema makes for larger than life stories from people who live ordinary lives.

The inspirational assent of someone who overcomes their personal demon or handicap, whether it's a runner with one leg or a blind musician, is a common movie theme. It doesn't have to be fancy or slick to succeed. An example is the Iranian movie of a son who wanted to leave his life of poverty to find world fame but finds success only when he returns home to save his father's restaurant.

Love and all its various forms dominate movie themes. Who can say that they ever know the answer to the questions posed by the complexities of a love relationship? Leave? Stay? Believe? Trust? Movies continually put characters into positions where they must choose a path. Maybe it's good for them, but bad for someone else? Which way is right? Where love is concerned, the cinema lines up on both sides of any issue. The moral dilemmas can be impossible:

Sophie's Choice, where Sophie is forced by the Nazis to make a horrific decision and save only one of her two children.

The world of anti-heroes has found its way into the movies. That means no more epic themes as in *Gone with the Wind*, with war, peace, love, loyalty, and endurance at its core. Now, an addict can be the main character as they battle for sobriety. Remember Jack Nicholson in *One Flew Over the Cuckoo's Nest*? Randle P. McMurphy was a nutty, everyman-type who led a rebellion from inside a psych ward to free people from the binds of brutal treatment like lobotomies. Who did not cheer for him? And who did not cheer for the blind, abandoned, and impoverished Ray Charles in *Ray*, where the man overcame his handicap to become a world-class musician?

What about female role models? Look at Julia Roberts as Erin Brockovich in the film of the same name. She took on the chemical company that was polluting the ground water and causing cancer. Or Meryl Streep as Karen Silkwood, one of the original whistleblowers. Sissy Spacek portrayed rags-to-riches country music star Loretta Lynn in *Coal Miner's Daughter*. These inspirational film characters are part of the fabric that forms "it". "It" can be found on screens from coast to coast. If you saw *RBG*, the story of Ruth Bader Ginsberg, you saw how one little woman was never going to be reduced by any gender issue brought about by men. When asked by a male interviewer how many women should be on the Supreme Court, she replied "Nine. It worked for you guys all these years—it's our turn."

Pick a movie—any movie—and let's see if it has "it'. I'll randomly choose the fourteenth most popular movie of all time, according to IMDb: 1954's *On the Waterfront,* starring Marlon

Brando, Eva Marie Saint, Karl Malden, Rod Steiger, and Lee J. Cobb. Directed by Elia Kazan. It's the story of a local prize fighter who took mob money to lose a fight. In return for the big score on their wagers, the bosses give him a "soft" job on the waterfront as a longshoreman. He witnesses another longshoreman's murder before he might possibly testify against the mob boss who controls the waterfront unions in Hoboken, New Jersey. His brother, Charlie, who is connected with the mob, looks out for him. Does he stand up and speak to the investigators, or does he stay "D&D" or "deaf and dumb" if anyone asks questions about the union. The "it" here is integrity and fearlessness in the face of corruption and injustice. The main character Terry Malloy can put himself in peril by talking to the investigators and then subsequently losing the only community he has, perhaps even lose his life. Or, he can remain "D&D" and life goes on the same, perhaps better if the bosses continue to reward him for his silence. A person comes away from the film asking himself, "What would I have done in Terry's shoes?"

The cinema is a teaching tool: in a matter of less than two hours, one can be presented with a moral or ethical dilemma that requires a difficult choice. How many college courses take forever to make the same point?

What it all comes down to is the artist expressing "it" via the medium of cinema—no different than the painter and his or her canvas. We the audience view the work and then we react. The best experiences are the ones where our emotions are engaged. If you want escape, then maybe the front seat of a giant rollercoaster will do it for you. Or maybe the scene in the African desert where the giraffes run free will make you happy. Some will cheer for the underdog Rocky as he yells, "Yo, Adrian! I did it!" Some will cry as the list of Schindler's survivors is flashed across the screen, with scenes of them walking with their relatives. Or, maybe you want to be quiet and reflective as the sun sets on any movie where love and good have prevailed.

Whatever your choice, if you come away having experienced a new thought or emotion, then you have experienced "it". A movie that "stays with you" is what the director is looking for—where the audience talks about the film for days to come. The writer/director has delivered "it" to you, and now it's your turn to do something with what you experienced. "It" is how movements are born.

The Theatre

Have you ever come out of the theatre after watching a really good play with the feeling that it changed you somehow? Maybe you understood something from a perspective you had never really thought about before? Or, you saw yourself as one of the characters and it either made you cringe or made you feel good about yourself.

Good theatre presents life in all its various, intricate forms. Lessons can be learned by many methods. I prefer laughter, as it's really the skill used in therapy to get people to see themselves in a different light. If you can laugh at yourself, you can admit your shortcomings, and that's the first step toward change.

If the character on the stage says he can and should be a better human being, and the characteristics he lists that need changing are yours as well, then he is doing the heavy lifting for you. If you can see him sympathetically, you can see yourself the same way.

Emoting in the audience is a form of identification and can be very powerful.

Prejudice can be identified in the theatre easier than at home. Characters point out hidden motivations, teachings, and folklore beliefs where it seems like everyday conversation, but the power comes from when the audience reacts the way the playwright intended. If you are the intended student, the lesson can be intense.

Remember all those confrontation encounter EST-type groups of the late sixties and early seventies? They were groups who formed with the intention of changing one's self-perception. Americans were in a phase of self-discovery, and these encounter groups were all the rage. The aim was to make people challenge themselves and become more honest and self-aware, which in turn would form a more harmonious society with the resulting self-responsibility and warmer view of one's neighbor. Differences were respected and invited inquiry, not ridicule. The encounter process exposed hidden fears.

The theatre loved it—it was a perfect forum for open discussion. The popularity of these groups changed theatrical format to include more audience participation: "Therapy in the Round", if you will. Add music, and the theatre set the tone for communication by emotive participation. I also saw the therapy fringe players jump on the bandwagon. Scream Therapy was letting out your bile, but it had short-term positive results—you still had to change if you wanted to feel better long-term.

I loved the long, drawn-out sagas in the theatre. Albee's *Who's Afraid of Virginia Woolf?* was a favorite. George and Martha, going at it like two warriors in an epic battle. Fair and foul, they got nastier the more they drank. They used sex as a weapon. They mocked innocence. They did everything to themselves and everyone else to get through the long night and reach the new dawn. How many times did the audience see themselves or their families in this ugly, slug-fest of a marriage? Failure, power, money, phoniness, jealousy, manipulation, threats, and cowardice were all on display—all on the table for the audience to feast upon. "Are you—or any part of you—on display here?"

The unsaid "it" is everywhere in the theatre. It doesn't have to be George and Martha slugging it out. It can be an Hispanic, one-man show with John Leguizamo laughing at his heritage in such a way that it makes it charming and funny. It's really teaching others to appreciate the different cultural aspects of family life. How can you not feel joy when Mexican comedian Paul Rodriguez puts you and ten family members in the *coche* to go get a chalupa? Or sit at the table of a huge Italian family for the Sunday meal, where they explain why it's not sauce, but gravy, to the guest? And Anthony always gets a slap on the back of the head. How about Jewish storytelling? The family member always receives groans at the beginning of the story, and applause or laughter at the end. Uncle Morris is seen from different perspectives to the joy and sometimes wincing of those hearing it for the first time. But "it" lives in all these scenes.

Try to tell a Chinese story without people eating. Impossible. The culture lives around the table, as do many others. If you are a good playwright, the table is always set. Ever watch *Bluebloods* on TV? The family cop Sunday Catholic dinner is as gritty as any real-life family drama. Themes of loyalty, integrity, conflict, respect, and ultimate consequences make for good theatre and good life lessons.

I saw Bruce Springsteen on stage, baring his soul and dispelling myths of fame and fortune. Such disarming honesty was cathartic for him as well as the audience. "No", he said, he was not a "working class hero". Matter of fact, he never, ever, had a job. He had a guitar and an alcoholic father. They went hand and hand. His ticket to "get out of Dodge" wasn't to get an education or learn to be a welder. He practiced his craft day and night, until he was good. Real good. Superstar good. But his biggest success was when his father came to see him after Bruce's son was born—and told him to be a better father than he was. They hugged for the first time. A real, long hug, with no words. Both men were reduced to tears. Powerful. An "it" connection.

How many young people in that audience were able to take away a poignant life message that might help them through their own struggles to find "it"? Failure is not an option if you are doing the thing you love: just do it well.

The one thing I love most about the theatre is the surprise element of discovery. You never really know what you are in for once the lights go down. It goes for almost any venue where you are the audience. It is the same with film and tv. Nowadays, it's the internet with podcasts and live-streaming. "It" is everywhere—you only need be receptive.

Music is "It". Period.

Music can capture an experience better than any other medium. It is totally inclusive of all our emotions and senses. There have been studies of catatonics in psych hospitals where spontaneous speaking has occurred when a certain song jars a memory to life. Savants have been shown to respond and remember every lyric to a song they heard in childhood. We can remember visually by being shown a picture. There are aromas that conjure up emotions and memories associated with that smell.

We can use touch to recall something familiar that is associated with a past event. But with music, "it" all comes rushing out in a burst of emotional memory. Nearly everyone has a list of special songs that can transport them back to the moment and setting where they heard it. Movies are made more emotionally powerful by their soundtracks. The combination of emotions people feel while watching a film is riveted into their souls by the music.

Music has been such a large part of my life, and the memories are my reward. We all have special songs, our emotional favorites. Let's explore this process.

Think of one of your favorite artists and play one of their songs in your head. I'll give you a pause here … where did it take you? Can you see where you were? Can you feel the emotion associated with it? That's the magic of "it" in music.

For example, I have two connections to one song. Let me set the scene: I am with a woman, both of us in our twenties, lying on a towel on the beach at one in the morning in Amagansett, East Hampton, New York. We are listening to The Rolling Stones singing "Midnight Rambler" on a portable cassette player, and we are going at it very heavily. I mean, the sand is flying every-where. For round two, we play the song again and now we start to time our movements to the song. Jagger is singing, "TALK-in' bout-the-MID-night-RAM-bler …" Boom! (Well, we timed the boom). The memory is intense as I recall it. *Boom!*

The second memory is the following year, 1970, at Madison Square Garden, when the young, passionate, hard-driving Rolling Stones were playing a three-and-a-half-hour concert. Jagger was at his best, prancing and flitting all over the stage. The lights went dark for about a minute, and when the spotlight came on, Mick appeared, wearing a red leather jacket. The music started and he drawled, "I'm talkin' 'bout the midnight rambler … *boom!*" Well, you can imagine what was happening with me. I "boomed" along with him. After that night, whenever I heard the song on the radio or played the record in my apartment, I merged the memories of seeing the Stones perform and the intense feeling from the beach. You want "it"? You have it all, right there.

I first heard Edith Piaf sing *"Non, je ne regrette rien"*—translated "I regret nothing"—at Googie's on Sullivan Street on the juke box. The orchestra began, *bamp-de-bamp-de-bamp-de-bamp* … then, Edith entered with the first verse: *"Non, je ne regrette rien …"* My reaction was immediate. *Who is that singing? What a beautiful voice!* Powerful, soulful, and hard-hitting. I learned she was a French jazz singer and she was called the "Little Sparrow" because of her diminutive size. I played the song repeatedly every time I was in the bar. It was such a perfect bar song, with the many customers who were lamenting over their beers. Edith was saying she had lost a lot, but she regretted none of it. So French!

When I worked at the White Horse, I made sure we got it on the juke box. They made a movie about her, *Le Vie en Rose*, in 2007 and it was a treat! I waited through the entire movie for her to sing it and they saved it for last. The song brings back my best memories from my Village years, as I see all the people who would sing along with her.

You could make your own emotional library of songs covering different periods of your life and the different music you listened to at that time. Did you ever notice how passionate people are about their music collections? They are the catalogs of their lives, through song.

I was lucky to be in New York in the late fifties to witness what is considered to be the last era of great jazz. Hanging at Charlie Parker's Birdland and seeing Miles Davis live was one of my peak moments. If you ever want a song to transport you to another place, listen to Miles Davis' "Saeta" from the *Sketches of Spain* album. It is the most trumpet you will ever hear. He puts you in Spain as the trumpet wails and the drums beat to the heat of the tundra. It marches on and by the end of the song, you are in another place.

During that period in New York, I saw and heard all the jazz greats: Thelonius Monk, Cannonball Adderley, Dave Brubeck, John Coltrane, Ahmad Jamal, John Lewis and the Modern Jazz Quartet, Ornette Coleman, Max Roach, Olatunji, Charlie Mingus, singers Peggy Lee and Nina Simone, just to name a few. When I hear those records now, I am transported back to the Village Gate, The Five Spot, the Blue Note, Basin St East, the Village Vanguard, the Half Note, and Smalls. It was a great time in jazz that quickly faded when the folk and rock explosion of the sixties began.

During the post-JFK years, the English mod scene erupted in the music industry, which was followed by the Beatles and the Stones and the onrush of British and then Hippie music. The American music scene exploded with both East and West Coast bands, along with the British scene, to take over from Memphis and Elvis. Music was king and the Fillmore East and West were the epicenters. Every Friday and Saturday night, the Fillmore East would rock with the best bands of that generation. I was there every Friday for the free concert in the afternoon in Central Park and then the night show at the Fillmore on 6th Street and 2nd Avenue.

To say I saw them all is accurate. From Frank Zappa and the Mothers of Invention to Janis Joplin, Jefferson Airplane, Jimi Hendrix, Canned Heat, Three Dog Night, LED Zeppelin, Quicksilver, The Band, Carlos Santana, Alvin Lee, Creedence Clearwater Revival, The Doors, Procol Harum, Van Morrison, Ravi Shankar, Steppenwolf, Buddy Guy, BB King, Traffic, Asleep at the Wheel, Country Joe and the Fish, Richie Havens, Lovin' Spoonful, Mamas and Papas, Jack Johnson, Johnny Winter, and on and on. The music at that time was where the street revolution was taking place. It was about freedom and stopping the war in Vietnam. It culminated in Woodstock and anyone who was there will tell you "it" was the pinnacle of the Hippie movement. Never were there more true words that covered that time in America than love, sex, and rock n' roll.

In the forties, I was a child in my parents' apartment and I listened to their music. My mother loved the Big Band era and Benny Goodman, Glenn Miller, Duke Ellington, Artie Shaw, Tommy Dorsey. Lionel Hampton and Count Basie were on the radio all the time. My memories are of a little brown radio that I had in my room that played all those bands, with my favorite being Benny Goodman's "Sing Sing Sing". My father liked the crooners: Frank Sinatra, Bing Crosby, Eddie Fisher, Dean Martin, Frankie Laine and Johnnie Ray. I liked Louis Prima, who sang with Keely Smith. He was fun and that appealed to me.

I listen to Middle Eastern and African music now, mostly Persian and Egyptian. Though I don't understand the lyrics, the instruments conjure up images of snake charmers and *casbahs*.

The Middle East has a rap culture also. Listen to "Desert Euphoria" by Giacomo Bondi or "Shab Ayum" by Turku; "Ancient Voices" and "Alibaba" by Karunesh, "Arabesque Lady" by Yousef Marakk, or the haunting "Orient Express" by Uzma. Also, "Oceans of Ecstasy" by Jehan. These musicians and their music possess an "it" you can get used to.

My Generation Had "It" and Lost it.

One of the saddest historical events I have witnessed was the loss of hope in my generation. We were the generation born either during or shortly after World War Two. We were children when the USA dropped the hydrogen bomb on Japan and killed hundreds of thousands of civilians in order to force that country to surrender. We were the first generation to go to school wearing dog tags for identification.

We grew up under Eisenhower, a popular Republican general from the war. We witnessed the growth and "good times" following the war. The suburbs grew and the television was a fixture in everyone's home. The USA was admired around the globe for saving France and the rest of Europe, including Germany, from the Nazis. We defeated Mussolini in Italy. The American family was the image seen on covers of the *Saturday Evening Post*. It was the time to buy your new washing machine or car. Communities sprang up on the edges of big cities as you could drive to work in your affordable car with twenty-cent gallons of gas.

As the fifties turned into the sixties, my generation started looking under the surface and what we saw was a deeply divided country between the haves and the have-nots. Segregation was in full view as people like George Wallace of Alabama and Ross Barnett of Mississippi defied federal law and stood in the doorways to prevent black students from entering schools. It was the time of Rosa Parks, who would not move to the back of the bus. It was the time for sit-ins at diners and marches with Dr. Martin Luther King, protesting states who had different tests for blacks in order to vote. We saw on national television the beatings of protesters in the streets outside the Democratic National Convention in Chicago. We saw the emergence of the Black Panther Party, who vowed to no longer take the beatings and fight back with violence if necessary. We saw an entire generation of people stand up for the planet with the first Earth Day. We witnessed women fighting for the Equal Rights Amendment, which unbelievably failed. We saw the riots in Detroit, Chicago, Los Angeles, Newark, and Plainfield as neighborhoods burned to the ground. We saw police beating homosexuals in Greenwich Village until the gay community emerged as one and stood up in the Stonewall riots.

The biggest marches were the ones that were aimed at stopping the War in Vietnam. Protesters chanted, "Hey, hey, LBJ! How many kids did you kill today?" The crowds grew in size and every newspaper was forced to report on the dissension. Universities led the way, with my alma mater being a major contributor as the students took over Columbia University while protesting Dow Chemical, who made napalm while the entire military industrial complex was supported by university research.

All this forced LBJ not to seek reelection. We saw the Federal troops tear gas protesters and charge at them on horseback at the Washington Moratorium. It was a time when a generation challenged the status quo which favored rich whites and suburbanites. It is the same today, where the right wing is in power and all its new laws are aimed at keeping the status quo as they refuse to see that the country is no longer white and Protestant and is now a mix of colors and ethnicities.

My generation was going to change it all. It was about free speech and the right to express one's opinion. It was the generation that was going to legislate for equality. The old boy network of Jim Crow would be ousted and replaced by civil equality and the courts would now reflect the changing mores. People would not go to jail for twenty years for having marijuana.

Then, everything came together in 1969 at Woodstock when 450,000 people spent a weekend together with music, rain, and pandemonium but no violence. It signaled a force for change.

Like all freedom movements, it attracted everyone. The fringe certainly showed up at Altamont in California the following year for the disastrous Rolling Stones concert where the Hell's Angels were hired as bodyguards and violence marred the event. It split the movement in two: how can a movement built on freedom and free expression now say there was no violent fringe? The counter-culture movement was based on freedom and permitted drugs to be its advertising. "Make Love not War" was a famous mantra and it included a joint. The reaction from middle America was strong as the troops came home from Vietnam. The politicians started changing drug sentencing laws to include much more severe punishment. The movement had failed by making drugs its centerpiece. Sure, the music was great and the concerts and street scenes attracted a lot of positive attention, but it ultimately brought down the message of freedom.

Once the downside of drugs was hitting the papers every week with another rock star overdosing, America's parents were duly alarmed over the dangers brought about by this movement. By the way, the ending of the Vietnam War was the greatest success of my generation. We also were successful in Washington with the passage of the Civil Rights and Voting Rights Acts. LBJ was a deeply torn President who could muster across-the-aisle support for his bills but had a huge blind spot when it came to Vietnam. The result was the election of the corrupt Richard Nixon after Robert F. Kennedy was assassinated.

The generations following mine were quiet and focused on themselves and making money. No one protested on the scale we had. The status quo returned and the Bush years took over. Except for a brief, liberal swing under the not-without-issues Bill Clinton, the country had dealt with its own issues only minimally. My generation got old and, instead of moving on with the new high-water mark set by electing the first black president, we elected a reactionary racist who is showing the right-wing supporters that the old guard is still in power. The rise of anti-immigrant fervor has fueled the prejudiced base of this President, whose one main goal is to eradicate the legacy of Barack Obama.

The streets now show some activity as children are protesting the Republican apathy to gun legislation. The insanity of American mass shooters goes unchecked by the power base, with the NRA funneling money to their legislators. It is now even uglier than the Nixon years, as money goes to the military and corporations and the country's citizens are gunned down while shopping.

We were supposed to gain after Obama, but we have failed and it is so sad. We now have a Russian-backed American president who is a white racist and a climate change denier. He believes in coal, oil, and gas and has destroyed all agencies that protected the planet and our citizens. We are now back to polluting the air and the water and gun control is not changing. This was the time when all the battles won in the streets were to manifest as political power; civil and social rights were to be more like what is seen in Northern Europe. The planet was to be protected. We warned everyone in the sixties that the oceans would rise, temperatures would increase, and the storms would get bigger and more destructive. It's all happening now, as we tolerate a person as president who cannot form a coherent sentence without a teleprompter and wants to drill in protected natural sanctuaries.

How did this happen? Were we blind to the racists who lay dormant and came out in force after they witnessed a black in the White House? Did we underestimate the power of a network like Fox News, which is a political tool of the Far Right? Did Rupert Murdoch and Roger Ailes control enough of the media to dupe its followers with misleading or patently untrue reporting into electing their puppet? Whatever the reason, including Russian interference and bots which show up on Facebook with false facts, the country is now in a terrible backslide. The mantra of "Great Again" shows no signs of greatness, only bigotry and stupidity at the top. My generation is now going to doctor visits and pushing their walkers. It's fifty years since Woodstock, and it feels like we need another one with an active generation of people who will rise to the occasion and say, "We aren't going to take it anymore." There are signs since the 2018 midterms that women and minorities have gotten the message about whom we've elected and are going to make sure it does not happen again.

I had hoped that my dreams and visions for a more humane and caring society would have been realized by now, and that we would be a country that would lead by example in the way we deal with our citizenry. We would have universal health care and Social Security would be realistic in what it pays back to its contributors. The need for the outlandish military would have been less as we worked for a more unified planet, which now is trying to survive our best efforts to destroy it. We are still dealing with the fact that capitalists are still in charge.

My generation would have found a way to educate children and teach them what they needed to know to be productive in their own futures. We would have figured out how to revere the elderly and their knowledge and not cast them aside as unproductive. I had imagined that by now corruption would have been taken away from politics, as the law would have banned corporate contributions. I would have hoped that the Electoral College would have seen its last day and gerrymandering would be out as well. Democracy calls for majority rule. You win if you get more votes. Simple. I had visions of racial and gender equality in social and work-related areas. You pay people by their skill level not their skin color or gender.

I still have some fight in me, and now is the time for all of us to stand up to the bigotry in charge of this country. I don't want to go out with "We lost 'it'". I want 'it' to be found once more.

"Last Call"

You have been there right? That time approaching when the bar is about to close and the bartender announces, "Last call". It is usually followed by some patron groans and then a mad scramble for their last chance to find someone for the night. Well, folks, we are now at the last call for "it". We have been on this journey for quite a time now, about fifty years' worth, and we have certainly seen the road, both rural and urban. It took us across America, talking to the big riggers as well as anyone sitting on a porch or bench. We have been in the therapy office, talking to men, women, kids and families. We talked with people in places like the general store, or in a metropolitan subway, or the courtroom, or a jail. We heard from street gang members and gay women bouncers. We talked with detectives and Army sergeants, porn stars and mountain scouts. We rode on an elephant's back, and hitched with gamblers, runaways, and farmers. We have looked at "it" from so many perspectives. We even tried to look "in" with the Buddhist. We certainly had a lot of coffee in diners with the wonderful waitresses, and we did try to talk to anybody and everybody who came across our path. Maybe this journey asked you some tough questions, or made you think about your own life and the choices you made or did not make. Possibly you were there with me when it was the good times and we were rolling along. Perhaps you shared the pain, or a tear or two, when life got rough. Now we stand here together and just for a moment, we ponder the future for a bit. Will you do anything differently? Will finding "it" be easier or harder as we go forward? Will you do it by yourself or will you get some help? Well, for me, I can't wait for the next conversation about "it" because this journey never stops. There is always somewhere new to go, and someone else to speak to, or maybe you will have that talk that will change you. Possibly the next time it's with me.

So, there you have it folks, the search for "it" and all its variations. My wish for you is that you have found "it" for yourself, and if not yet, then someday in the future, along your path. Enjoy this search, and maybe tell whomever you meet on the way, about a guy you read, who spent a whole lifetime searching for "it".

If you want to be a Therapist

If you are someone who wants to be a therapist, you must start by wanting to learn the craft to the best of your ability. You also have to commit to a personal psychotherapy. You really should not sit in the "big chair" until you have sat in the other one. Your journey will be to learn "it". First things first. For me, it was learning psychology. I started with the big boys: Sigmund Freud, Carl Jung, Erich Fromm, Karen Horney, Sándor Ferenczi, Harry Stack Sullivan and Erik Erickson, to get a basic understanding of the psychoanalytic theory and the application of the concepts of *Id*, *Ego,* and *Superego*. Once I understood the unconscious and its various forms, I could move on to learning the ego defense mechanisms. I read Wilhelm Reich for an understanding of character analysis and the wonderful theory of "character armor". After that light reading, I took a sidestep and read Margaret Mead, who found similarities with Jung in tribal communities and the way they formed societal norms and used universal symbols.

Next would be the psychologists who focused on how we learn and what we learn. I loved Gestalt theory from the experimental Berlin School: field perspective and integration of thought from known and unknown sources. The Behaviorists were next: Watson, Pavlov, BF Skinner and G. Stanley Hall to Albert Ellis, Piaget, and Binet. Most of these theorists are similar or blend in most cases. From the relations theorists, I would add Carl Rogers, Fritz Perls, and Abraham Maslow, whose Actualization theories mirrored the deeper theories of Jung, who talked about when a man who represents only himself becomes the Man to represent all of Mankind. Simple stuff—ten to fifteen years should cover its learning and application.

I had started with psychoanalytic theory as a teenager figuring out his dreams, and that was also in play years later at Columbia University, as their psych courses in Abnormal and Personality Development relied heavily on that perspective. But an interesting dualism appeared in their other classes. There was this basic Social Work theory of a person in a situation configuration. It translated into the inner person living within an organized system of family and community. Roles were learned and repeated. It became harder and harder for me to apply the 19th century, basically male-dominated, authoritarian Austrian psychoanalytic theory to modern-day America. The role of women had changed dramatically, and the role of family was significantly altered, especially for African Americans who were torn from their families by slavery and its aftermath. Eastern Asians also seemed excluded.

The effects of poverty on families and their values was what I was seeing every day on the streets of New York's Lower East Side, where gangs were the ruling social norm. Split and divorced families with no dad or two moms in an extended family were more common than the traditional Freudian model. Kids raising kids was also common. I understood that Freud's theory applied to internal psychodynamics, but not any longer to social norms.

What made sense to me now were the theories of Family Therapy, where people of any gender could play a significant role in the development of a family and its values. Two dads or two moms was different, but it worked. The idea of extended families with split roles was more complicated, but the kids seemed to figure it out. Families speaking two or three languages did not confuse the kids. It made more and more sense to me that broken families were raising normal kids. There was a common ground application of systemic thought that helped me understand poverty, illness, and survival. It had nothing to do with penis envy or hysteria.

I then read Salvador Minuchin, Alfred Adler, Nathan Ackerman, Harry Aponte, Gregory Bateson, Milton Erickson, R.D. Laing, Ivan Boszormeny-Nagy, Murray Bowen, Virginia Satir, Jay Haley, Chloe Madanes, Mara Selvivni Palazzoli (Milan School), Lynn Hoffman, John Weakland, Carl Whitaker, and Lyman Wynne, to name some of the leaders of family theory. They were kind-hearted hair-splitters when it came to differentiating one theoretical position from the other, but they were all family theorists when an analyst was in the room. Like Jews debating which form of Judaism should prevail, they'll never agree, but when an Arab enters the conversation, they are all Jews.

The combined knowledge of all these family theorists said

that family, no matter in what form, was the essential guidepost for what a child would learn. On the spectrum from healthy and productive to addictive and violent, a child would learn to emulate or escape, depending on their own internal and external opportunities. Poverty produces both astronauts and addicts. Some can learn to overcome the situation in which they are born—others cannot. Despite one's surroundings, a healthy, role-defined, and productive family offers the best chance for survival.

I learned there was no substitute for learning your craft, whether you were a race car driver, electrician, detective, farmer, or therapist. For the therapy part I had individual and group; it took years, and periodically I would return for issues that emerged. I had continual supervision, even after I was providing it. Learning never stops. In this profession, like many others who deal with life and death issues of the public at large, you need to know what you know—and what you don't. Enjoy the journey, it may lead you to "it".

Lightning Source UK Ltd.
Milton Keynes UK
UKHW010719250520
363803UK00001B/77